The Challenges of English Second Language Teachers and Learners

FOCUS ON LINGUISTIC ASPECTS OF ENGLISH LANGUAGE

G. Indira

ISBN 979-8-89322-254-8

Debates On English Introduction

Discussions On English Medium

Difficulties in English Acquisition

TELANGANA RESIDENTIALEDUCATIONAL INSTITUTIONS SOCIETY &

Ch.Ramana Kumar, M.Sc., B.Ed.
Secretary, TREI Society

I would like to congratulate and commend Smt. Indira on her efforts in publishing The Challenges of English Second Language Teachers and Learners. She has made an effort to illustrate the challenges that bilingual pupils encounter. Her resolutions are based on her observations as an English teacher from the outside world and her experiences in the classroom, but not on conjecture. She has made an effort to clarify the drawbacks of those strategies and tactics as well as the viability a using them in the classroom. Aft' providing an overview of the English language, the book discuss. numerous ways and technique for teaching the language. To support her theories, she enrolled in many English language courses at reputable universities. I admire how the author created this masterpiece under the epidemic lockdown. This book offers helpful advice on how to improve proficiency of the students in the English Language. Both teachers of the English language and the enthusiasts of English education should read it.

Best wishes!

Secretary
SECRETARY
Telangana Residential Educational
Institutions Society (Regd.)
HYDERABAD-500 001.

Ms. Indira has come up with her book which gives a glimpse of English Language Teaching scenario in Telugu states. Having experience as a classroom teacher, material developer and administrator Ms. Indira has documented very useful anecdotes that come to her direct experience or from contemporary events. She extensively contributed in material preparation during stay in SCERT. She has been continuing her passion of writing articles on various topics in different journals and blogs. I hope this book will be useful material in English Language Teaching (ELT) for researchers, teachers and institutions. This book is the first of its kind in the field of teaching English at school level in Telugu states by an experienced teacher.

Dr. Jani Reddy Pandiri - Lecturer- Govt DIET Ranga Reddy, Vikarabad. Telangana state.

Contents

Abbreviations

L1	Language-1 - Mother Tongue/Regional Language
L2	Language-2 - Here English (any other language other than L1)
L3	Language-3 - (In some states of India Hindi is L2 & English L3)
ESL	English Second Language
ELT	English Language Teaching
ESLT	English Second Language Teaching
GELT	Global English Language Teaching
GE	Global English
SLA	Second Language Acquisition
SLL	Second Language Learners
UG	Universal Grammar
CCE	Continuous Comprehensive Evaluation
TET	Teacher Eligibility Test
DSC	District Selection Commission
UPSC	Union Public Service Commission
AI	Artificial Intelligence
A.P.	Andhra Pradesh (State)
ASER	Annual Status of Education Report
NEP2020	New Education Policy 2020
NCF2005	National Curriculum Framework 2005
NCF2023	National Curriculum Framework 2023

NCERT	National Council of Educational Research and Training
SCERT	State Council of Educational Research and Training
LSRW	Listening, Speaking, Reading and Writing
CPD	Continuous Professional Development
UNESCO	United Nations Educational, Scientific and Cultural Organisation

Preface

My experiences in English Language Teaching (ELT), as an English Second Language (ESL) learner in school education and teacher in profession, I have put forth in this book candidly. I observed difficulties in ELT, while teaching to the regional/mother-tongue (Telugu) medium students. As a matter of fact, English is the third language to my students. Yet, it is considered to be L2. For, in the state of United Andhra Pradesh and Telangana, the school educational institutions follow the three-language formula, proposed by the Union Government, soon after the Independence of the country. According to the formula, the regional language becomes the L1, Hindi-L2 and English-L3 within the state. While teaching, I was keen on observing the learner's difficulties. Being an employee of A.P. Residential Schools, I had to spend most of my day time and also a few hours at night monitoring schoolchildren in their studies. Hence, on an average my hours of work and watching of schoolchildren had been much more than a standard school teacher. I was more fortunate to have so much scope and leverage for observation within the classroom and outside the instructional hours. That has led to thoroughness in observation. This book is a comprehensive work on linguistic aspects of English language teaching for school teachers, English education enthusiasts and for the inquisitive public in general on education and educational reforms.

In this book I dealt with what I investigated in my own mini- research way, starting from the history of English in India to: linguistically how English language is structured i.e. structuralism, different methods and approaches of ELT and how practically they are feasible/not feasible, some problems posed by high school learners in English grammar, as a teacher of ELT my doubts regarding the subject, mother-tongue medium and its usefulness in primary education, bilingual method, multilingualism's need in India and also Covid-19- technology based English education. In conclusion, I added snippets on: Phillipson's English Imperialism, Monolingual-English classroom, Englishes i.e., Global Englishes,

Translanguaging and multilingual English Teaching. The aim is to highlight English education in India and the feasibility of acquiring the language for the first-generation learners. My efforts and endeavour are to enlighten through my presentation, some of the aspects of teaching English, problems encountered and suggested remedies, to other teachers of English from my side and for the grasp of the general public.

In teaching my students or equipping myself with the latest skills and developments in the English language, I left no stone unturned. So as to improve myself as a teacher and teach well I did several courses viz. PGCTE, PGDTE and M.Phil. in English (the field of study being: Linguistics and Phonetics), all of them are from none other than the reputed Central Institute of English and Foreign Languages (CIEFL) now known as English and Foreign Languages University (EFLU), Hyderabad. My inquisitiveness and my education in EFLU made this book possible.

G. Indira (aka K. Indira)

Hyderabad.

Introduction

I am a retired Post Graduate Teacher (PGT in English) who worked in Andhra Pradesh (united) and Telangana Residential Schools under TREIS (Telangana Residential Educational Institutions Society). I have an experience of more than twenty-five years in teaching English to high school students. This book is written out of my own experience as a teacher of English and how I felt while teaching the English-subject and what are the difficulties of students. This book deals with the linguistic aspects of English and is helpful to English teachers to know about the language. It is also meant for the general public that are keen on knowing the English language difficulties. My own experiences coupled with students' dilemmas about the language are explained vividly in some chapters of the book. They are all written by hands-on experience. Generally, researchers touch upon teaching items by analysing each academically. In this book how practically, students take or think about the language-items is shown.

The book begins with the history of the introduction of the English language and moves on to the teaching methods and approaches. English language teaching methods and approaches have been changing from time to time. For, each method or approach has its own limitations. In the later chapters linguistic evolution and based on which, how English language could be taught is dealt with. These chapters are meant to arouse curiosity among English teachers. Usually, ESL classes are run on a Bilingual method. Multilingualism is rare, as India has carved out linguistic states. However, there are border states, where intermingling of languages takes place. Similarly, migration and urbanization of people has led to a multilingual atmosphere. Hence, there is a need for a multilingual approach to teaching English. The recent pandemic Covid-19 has brought disruption to conventional teaching. This disruption has given momentum and impetus to technological advancement. The technological advantages of Covid-19 period in teaching of English are a part of this book. Apart from that, the latest on-going debates in teaching of English all over the world viz. Monolingual-English classroom, Englishes i.e. Global Englishes, Translanguaging and Multilingual English Teaching have been discussed.

This book is a product of my toil during the two-years of Covid-19 Pandemic period. The lockdown-leisure, the minimal social interaction accrued time to read vast materials of English language teaching. In addition, tediously attending long Zoom-meets of eminent persons of authority in English to grab a point or two that challenges my thought -process. While teaching English in school, I continued to do courses to update myself. They include the Post Graduate Certificate Course in English (PGCTE), Post Graduate Diploma Course in English (PGDTE) and M.Phil. in English (in the field of: Linguistics and Phonetics). All three courses I did were from the English and Foreign Languages University (EFLU), Hyderabad. Hence, this book is the result of my cumulative effort of teaching and research. Wish this distillation of my experience and knowledge would come handy to at least some teachers of English and the other interested sections.

My whole effort in writing this book was to explain English could be learnt by Indian students but it cannot be caught as a language ('language should be caught, not taught' is a famous quote). For, they have no such environment outside their school. Anyhow, whatever they learn is enough as a working knowledge in their real-life situations. For those in Information Technology (IT), they need somewhat more than that of normal citizens, as they need to express to the outside world and understand what they get as input from them. Hence, they require more language and more expression. In any case, there are ways and means to learn English from outside the school system. The book is more argumentative in making for and against English language promotion in India. Of course, the proof of the pudding is in eating it. So, therefore it is for the readers to judge.

Chapter Wise-Summary

This book includes fifteen chapters, broadly each dealing with a subject related to English language teaching or learning in the ESL context.

Chapter-1. Historical Aspects - Pros and Cons on the Introduction of English

This chapter contains: from pre-Independent India till date, the debates and discussions that have gone on, in introducing English in schools as a language and as medium of instruction. The relationship between language and culture: would English language influence the culture of India? And what is culture all about? - are discussed.

Chapter-2. Methods, Approaches & Drawbacks

Almost all teachers know which method or approach has to be taken up at what time considering the classroom situation. Each method/ approach has its own limitations/ drawbacks. In this chapter, there are comprehensive deliberations on methods, approaches and their fault lines.

Chapter-3. Different Syllabuses and Modes of Teaching

The evolution of syllabus and approaches to teaching of English are talked about. Content-based syllabus was followed earlier in the 1960s and 70s. Later academic realization was that, that it would not lead to language use i.e. language-communication. Hence, task-based learning and communicative-approach have come into place. Now, to what extent the present syllabus caters to the needs of students? – has been the subject matter.

Chapter-4. As English Second Language Teacher- Difficulties Faced

Many in India agree that the knowledge in English is beneficial. So, to learn the English language students would leave no stone unturned. For them, the easiest way to get marks is to mug some standard answers from prescribed reading passages/lessons given in text to produce the same in the examination. To write on their own is very difficult. The English language vocabulary and structure/grammar are extensive. Hence, students' difficulties in each grammatical item are dealt with.

Chapter-5. English Only as a Subject in School - Difficulties of students

For most schoolchildren in India, who pursue studies in their mother tongue or regional language, English as a subject is difficult, after mathematics. Of course, mathematics is a knowledge subject and English is a skill-based one. For understanding and solving problems in mathematics intellect is needed. But acquiring the skills of English, aptitude and exposure to the language are in a way the prime requisites. The various doubts expressed by students in the English class, while learning the language, makes an English teacher wonder. Some of them are presented here. Two-case studies of grown-up students regarding their opinion are also taken into consideration.

Chapter-6. Language is for self-expression

For any child to write something basic in his mother tongue is not a problem. This most students can do, what they cannot do is to write well or effectively or impressively presenting all the views in mind. So, the L 1, teachers seek effectiveness. For an English teacher (of L 2/L 3) to expect from students both: basic-writing in English and advanced skills of writing, is a far-fetched dream. If a student cannot communicate properly either in spoken or written form, She/he cannot express herself/himself properly. Therefore, language is not only to communicate with others but also for self-expression.

Chapter-7. Primary Education – Importance of Mother Tongue

Introducing English-subject (as the second language) from class-1 onwards is not a subject matter of discussion anymore in all states in India. However, to have English as a medium of instruction right from primary education in state government-run schools, that cater to the poor and downtrodden, is a drastic step. The states have no such ecosystem for English learning to take place. Suppose, a government school child is asked to name ten birds or ten animals or ten flowers or plants, she would immediately name in her mother-tongue. Because, they are in the child's lexicon. Hence, primary education in mother-tongue/regional language is less stressful to a child.

Chapter-8. Preference to English Medium of Instruction-Reasons

Why are the underprivileged sections latching on to English medium for their child's progress? Why can't they get the same progress with regional mediums, where the student's mother tongue plays a big role in understanding the subject-knowledge taught? - are the questions. To which answers/reasons are debated.

Chapter-9. Introduction of English Medium-Opposing views

The premise on which the advocates of mother tongue/home language medium argue is: linguistic or emotional interaction is the foundation for mother tongue. The dominant discourse of the second language (English) never acknowledges this. Yet, on the ground people moved away from those premises. - elaboration on that topic.

Chapter-10. English Second Language Students-Practical Difficulties in Speaking

Once (this was in the year 2005), it so happened, I asked my students of class IX (Telugu Medium learners of English with a rural background) to give a 2-minute talk on their dearest friend. I even provided simple guidelines for them to speak … To me it was astonishing to hear their talk and language disabilities in their utterances. It was so alarming, after sometime; I started noting down their sentences to analyse what went wrong in their grammar. The sample sentences of their speech-analysis were presented.

Chapter-11. Bilingualism in ELT

Many academicians of English oppose the use of mother-tongue/regional-language in the English class simply because the target-language i.e., English will not get due attention and is neglected. Nevertheless, in most of the mother tongue/regional medium schools, the bilingual method is used in teaching English. This has many reasons.

Chapter-12. Multilingualism in ELT

Linguistic diversity in India is a unifying factor. The unifying thread is the culture. The same cultural values are expressed in different languages. That is the reason the Sahitya Akademi that was set-up soon after Independence as central nodal agency for all Indian-language-literatures contains the motto: *"Indian literature is one, written in many languages,"* shows the innate unity in all Indian languages.

Chapter-13. The Necessity of Multilingualism in the Present Scenario

(Endangerment to world and Indian Languages - Danger is Looming Large)

At present, English is looming large all over the world and in India, making the native languages small. Hence, the trend of teaching English has been changing in accordance with the time into the multilingual culture. In multilingual countries, the course correction is: to encourage the indigenous languages along with English.

Chapter-14. Assessment of ESL Acquisition through Examinations

'These exams (meaning to say competitive entrance examinations for joining in professional courses) also force students to learn a very narrow band of material in a single stream, rather than allowing the flexibility and choice that will be so important in the individualized education system of the future.' - That was pointed out in National Education Policy 2020 with regard to competitive examinations. Students that study for general examinations also do not go by wide and flexible reading. They often go by narrow question banks to pass the examinations. Hence, they do not acquire in-depth knowledge or understanding of the subject.

Chapter-15. Covid-19 Pandemic - Innovative English Teaching

In Covid-19 pandemic affected years (2020-22) English teachers heavily relied on technology. Those teachers that are not tech-savvy also learnt how to use it. It is the sheer imperative that drove them to learn tech-devices to teach. There are many hidden aspects of the teaching-learning process that came to forefront. One of them is, an English teacher's pronunciation. The pronunciation of most of the teachers is accented with their L1 to a great extent. Insisting on pronunciation to be correct as native-English speaker- like is too ambitious. But towards that end with accent neutral is possible.

Conclusion-Snippets

Latest on-going debates and discussions on English

1. English Imperialism

Phillipson's arguments - the global teaching of English was an act of linguistic imperialism etc. and how they were dispelled by other scholars.

2. Native Speakers Teaching English

The ideology of native speakers' ownership of language is more seriously questioned today than ever before – how is it? For and against arguments.

3. Monolingual English Classroom

Monolingual ESL classes use only English and no other language. These are basically English-alone classrooms. Again pros and cons.

4. Multilingualism

Prof Ajit K Mohanty has done pioneering work in multilingualism. He says, because of the formation of linguistic-language-states in India (soon after Independence) the dominance of 'one' language i.e. the language spoken in the state has pushed the minor languages to the edge…hence multilingual approach would revive the minor languages. - Feasibility issues are discussed.

5. Global Englishes (GE)

English-speakers in non-native countries are seeking recognition of their varieties on par with that of the native-English.

6. Translanguaging

Students read the text in English and discuss it in another language either their mother tongue or regional language. That's translanguaging. Specifying the benefits of it.

Chapter-1

Historical Aspects --- Pros and Cons on the Introduction of English

The debates and discussions on introduction of English education predates Indian Independence. Even during the British colonial rule, there was a stiff opposition to the introduction of English education in India. At present, many opponents of English education hold Babington Macaulay to be the culprit for the English education in the country. There is a reason for this argument. For Macaulay's famous minutes of Education in 1831, stoutly defended the need for English education (in India) by deriding indigenous languages, especially Sanskrit. "Minute on Indian Education" ([1831–1853] 1935, pp. 345-361), which proposed English as the principal language of instruction for any national system of education in India, so that western science, culture, and technology could more easily be transmitted.

'Macaulay's Minute on Indian Education (1835) argued that English should be the language of instruction, against Orientalists, who favoured Arabic and Sanskrit rather than vernacular languages. Late-twentieth-century postcolonial studies have revived interest in Macaulay's role in this debate.'[1] Macaulay felt Indian literature to be of no worth. However, in a true sense, the introduction to English was made possible later, by the reformist Viceroy-General of the British Empire Lord Bentinck. Even today, the Indian Constitution does not list English as one of the languages of the Union. Only the Sahitya Academy of India recognises English. The Academy has an Advisory Board for English.

Late (Prof.) K. R Srinivasa Iyengar is the authority in English literature in India. In the introduction of his book *Indian Writing in English*, the importance of English is thus stated: 'But for all-India administration, inter-state communication, pursuit of knowledge at higher levels, and for maintaining and promoting international contacts, English is providing an indispensable tool, a cementing force, a key, and a channel all at once.'[2] He also stated, 'the English language to be like the Suez Canal for the intellectual linkage between the West and the East. The Indian thought from Vedic to modern times has found its way to the West. The eminent Indian thinkers ... from Rammohan Roy and Keshub Chunder Sen to Vivekananda, Tagore, Sri Aurobindo, Gandhi and Radhakrishnan ... have made themselves heard in the West.[3]. In this context, the mention of the Suez Canal is note-worthy. To know: the Suez Canal is a man-made waterway (opened in 1869) connecting the Mediterranean Sea to the Indian Ocean. It enables a more direct route between Europe and Asia. Before this route was established, Europeans had to circumnavigate the African continent. Hence, it was a direct and easy route to the western countries from the East. This free passage enabled by the Suez Canal is vital for international trade and travel. In the same way, the English language works for international relationships, as a vital link between the East and the West.

According to Randolph Quirk, 'Some of its (English's) present importance, however, oddly results from the large number of other languages available in India ... Hindi, Bengali, Tamil, Telugu, Gujarati, Kannada and several others, each spoken by millions of people. When India became independent in 1947 it was decided to make Hindi the national language...English was given equal status temporarily. It was then intended that English should cease to be one of the two official languages in 1965, but when 1965 came, the Indian Government ... in the face of bloodshed in Madras and elsewhere ... had to give assurances that English would continue as a working language for official purposes.'[4] That is how the continuance of English has taken place. But the apprehension in some quarters is: English-speaking people in India follow the English cultural-moors. Undoubtedly, any language with it brings its culture. As you are aware many of us greet each other with a 'good morning', 'good afternoon', 'good evening/good night', and also as a matter of courtesy and etiquette, most of us say: 'thank you', 'please', 'sorry' etc. These mannerisms started nearly two centuries ago. Of course, they were all urban-centric. Srinivasa Iyengar writes, 'Western ways ... in manners and customs, in dress, in eating, in salutation ... became current in the bigger towns and cities ...1835 to 1855.'[5] Pointing to same period of introduction of

English, Iyengar opines, 'All the same, the trite metaphor of the West impinging on India is apt to be misleading. English education was a new force … part elixir, part poison … injected into Indian life, but the immediate effects were seen only on the surface.'[6]

Now, one may get a doubt, as to what is culture and how does a language get the culture of the native land with it? Culture is a broad term. It could be defined in many ways. To put it in a nutshell, 'culture' is a system of behaviour and attitudes that are valued in particular language and land. However, Raymond Williams in his essay on 'The Analysis of Culture'[7], categorizes culture into three levels. The first being an ideal one of high-order. In which, culture is a state of human perfection in terms of certain absolute and universal values. This could be easily understood in the way we describe a person. If a person cheats or lies or behaves rudely or foul-mouths, we attribute it to his cultural upbringing. Similarly, if a person has decent behaviour and etiquette, we laud his cultural moorings. The second definition of culture, according to R Williams, is a body of intellectual and imaginative work…nature of thought and experience…the details of the language, form and convention in which these are active…described and valued. This is true, when Indian painting, music and Indian novels written in Indian languages and nuances are easily understood by Indians. Here along with the language and thought process, the national context also plays a role. The third and the most important one given by him is the: 'social' definition of culture. According to which, culture is a description of a particular way of life, which expresses certain meanings and values not only of art and learning but also in institutions and ordinary behaviour. English as a language brings this (social definition of culture) to Indians, is one of the anxieties expressed by the opponents of the English language. However, almost all Indians are unanimous, in this present-day world, that English is most needed. The debates over the English language now are on: when to introduce? How much? And at what level in the school education?

The traditional wisdom found in all Indian languages is part of Indian cultural heritage. It includes, 'oral history, poetry, epic tales, creation stories, jokes, riddles, wise sayings, and lullabies. These genres—the product of human ingenuity, wordplay, and creativity—may be found in all languages.'[8] Indians should be mindful not to lose their own languages' culture, which is quintessentially theirs, while adopting English language. The latest National Curriculum Framework (NCF) 2023 also emphasizes language-culture relationship. It says, 'Language does not operate in isolation and is related to social interaction, context, and culture. Language development among students is the act of cultural development; it invariably requires learning about its culture and society.'[9]

Of course, nowadays, there are many English-educated Indians that are rooted in Indian culture. When we study language and culture as two interconnected issues, language does impact culture. However, in India, English is indigenised. There are writers of old vintage: Mulk Raj Anand, R.K. Narayan, Raja Rao and the recent Vikram Seth, Chetan Bhagat etc. depict Indian culture and Indian thought to the world. Aurobindo who studied in England in English right from his childhood has found his attraction in Indian thought. So, foreign culture prevailing over Indian culture is a far-fetched thought.

Indeed, India's success in software is due to the knowledge in English. But that itself is not everything. There are people with scant spoken English-knowledge who could do well in software, as they have expertise in technical knowledge. Strangely, some could read and comprehend the technology written in English but unable to express it orally in the English language. Indisputably, knowledge in English helps technical personnel to express themselves and their work, when they communicate how they were able to do so and so program successfully, or to appraise what they had done in their job, they do need English fluency. Because they are talking to their peer-groups and their bosses that are English-speaking most often.

Proficiency in English could be acquired outside the school education curriculum also, as there are many institutions online and offline available in India. There is no dearth of apps and social media channels to get exposed to English and for students to clear their doubts. English in India is a window of opportunity to know the world and work in the global system. No amount of western culture could replace the eastern culture and vice versa. The advocates of culture need not be apprehensive, as English remains an Indian language in a multilingual atmosphere. 'English does not stand-alone, … English needs to find its place with other Indian languages in different states'.[10] That is the reason for stressing on multilingual teaching in the English classroom.

1. https://www.encyclopedia.com/people/history/historians-miscellaneous-biographies/thomas-babington-macaulay

2. KR Srinivasa Iyengar 1995, Introduction, Indian Writing in English, Sterling Publishers Pvt. Ltd., New Delhi-110016, p.13

3. Ibid p.15

4. Randolph Quirk, The Use of English, Orient Longman 1995 p.12

5. KR Srinivasa Iyengar 1995, Introduction, Indian Writing in English, Sterling Publishers Pvt. Ltd., New Delhi-110016, p.29

6. Ibid p.29

7. Raymond Williams-The Analysis of Culture, Cultural Theory And Popular Culture, A Reader, second edition, The University of Georgia Press 30602, Athens, Published in the United States of America 1998. p.48

8. K. David Harrison 2007, When Languages Die: The Extension of The World's Languages And The Erosion of Human Knowledge, Swarthmore College Libraries' Works. p.17

9. National Curriculum Framework for School Education (NCF)-2023, NCERT, p. 136

10. National Curriculum Framework (NCF) 2005, National Council for Educational Research and Training, New Delhi p.58

Chapter-2

Methods, Approaches & Drawbacks

Let us see what are the methods and approaches English teachers adopt while teaching in the class. No method/approach is foolproof. Yet, they have to be known, understood and practiced in the classroom by all teachers. Almost all teachers know which method or approach has to be taken up, at what time, considering the classroom situation. Each method or approach has its own limitations, which you can call them drawbacks. In this chapter, we will discuss comprehensively about the methods, approaches and their fault lines.

i. Grammar-Translation Method to Structural Method

In the past, English had been taught in India using the Grammar-Translation Method'. It is the oldest method of teaching. It was the impression of academicians then that knowing grammar of a language thoroughly gives confidence in speaking and writing. Fundamentally, the grammar of a second language provides the rules of the language. For any game or sports, knowing the rules of the game are important before playing. Unless you have the rules at hand, you cannot apply, is the principle. So, for generations together Grammar-based language teaching continued. In India, many young and old have mastered the rules of grammar from the famous: Wren and Martin Grammar Book. They used to almost by heart the entire rule-based grammar in it. Their grammar was so perfect and immaculate that they could even challenge the native speaker of English on parsing a sentence. Some of them were well-versed with all Shakespeare's plays and could repeat lines at length from them eloquently. However, most of them could neither speak English nor write it fluently. For, they were not accustomed to having an English-speaking environment around. So, their conversational language also appeared more cultivated than natural.

Of course, the grammar-translation method did not remain with the teaching of grammar alone. The method also took care of reading, writing and translation. During the correction of the examination papers, grammatically correct and well-structured sentences were awarded marks, and ill-constructed sentences were struck down. Translation from English to mother tongue, precis- writing, and proverb expansion were some of the questions then for testing. They were all to test writing skills. Not much emphasis was given to listening or speaking in that method. That method was all for literary mastery rather than for the communication of language. Mostly English text and language was learnt by rote memorisation. The teaching of the text was through translation into the mother tongue i.e., regional language. Yet, some people that studied in the age-old grammar translation method topped the competitive examinations like that of civil services and acclaimed laurels.

The later realization was, merely knowing rules of grammar and loading vocabulary in mind would not lead to fluency in the language. The English language has to be constantly used. The ability to use the language grows by practice. After all, 'practice makes a man perfect 'is an old adage. To be able to speak or gain knowledge in English, academicians proposed teaching English in English would be better. This method is known as: Direct Method of teaching English, where the student needs to understand from English to English, but not through vernacular. That way, they could get exposure and immersion in the English language. For this to happen, a teacher should know the language well. Even now, this method is followed in elite English medium schools. Whereas in other schools, particularly in regional vernacular medium schools, the Bilingual Method is followed. The bilingual method is in between the grammar-translation method and the direct-method. That is, taking from both but striking a balance. Other than these basic-methods, there are other methods like: the Natural Method, The Phonetic Method, The Audio-lingual Method, Activity Method, Situational Method and of course, The Direct Method, but they do not cater to all English language skills adequately.

What is a "method of teaching" in a true sense? A method of teaching is a way in which teaching is done. It includes: 'the tasks that the teacher does in the classroom and also curriculum, course-book, teaching techniques, the context of teaching and the refinement of testing procedures. As such teaching is a multidimensional process.'[1] What is the best method? The best method of teaching English is the one, which develops all the four language skills: Listening, Speaking, Reading and Writing (LSRW). The best method is supposed to be a "complete" method that covers all four skills. Apart from methods, there are several approaches for teaching the English language. Like methods, they keep on progressing as per the research on language teaching. What is an approach? An approach is the way in which a subject is approached or dealt with. Nowadays, we have technology-driven methods to learn English. English for specific purposes (job-oriented ones) are also available.

Since, all the methods failed to teach the four language skills LSRW, by and large, there was a search for the appropriate approach to deal with the problem. The first and foremost came to place was the structural approach to English teaching replacing the grammar-based one. That is, proper structures of English are needed for the learners (mainly of second language) to learn. Grammar tells the rules you need to know about the language to gain native-like competence in the language. Is this not sufficient? While learning grammatical sentences, structures are in-built. Wouldn't it suffice? It would not seem to be the case. Observe a child acquiring your own language. While acquiring language, the child will observe people around her using language and a set of expressions. These sets of expressions are the structures. Languages are structure-dependent. Every language has its specific structures. Hence, learning English needs learning or acquiring its basic-structures.

Consequently, advocates of structural approach/structuralism, all over the world, raised objections to the grammar-based teaching and learning of English, by citing many fallacies in it. Among them, the main fallacy is the Latinate fallacy, i.e., English follows Latin grammar which is not specific to the English language. The Latin grammarians mostly depended upon the Greek modal for the description of Latin. Like our Panini for Sanskrit grammar, Plato, the Greek philosopher who took on the subject of grammar seriously. Here, the advocates of structuralism, assumed that each language has its own unique structure and must be described in its own terms. They also questioned why some academicians use meaning to explain grammatical structure (i.e. grammar-translation). For, a language teacher of any Indian language, teaches the grammar of the language almost technically i.e. what is what in a sentence, as the meaning is tacitly understood.

The proponents of the structural approach also blamed traditional grammar for its lack of explicitness. They, unlike the traditional grammarians that laid much emphasis on the written form of language, attached more importance to speech. To put it in a nutshell, the traditional grammarians were prescriptive (giving importance to form) and the structural ones were descriptive (giving prominence to meaning). Interestingly to compare both and contrast them, it is said, 'both the prescriptive and descriptive grammarians make use of "rules". The prescriptive grammarians' rules, like the laws of the government, tell people what they ought to do. The descriptive grammarian's rules, like the laws of physics or biology, describe what actually happens or is done.'[2] Therefore, the important criteria to evaluate grammar adequacy is that of the descriptive adequacy.

1.   HNL Sastri, Lesson-1: Principles of Language Teaching-1990, PGDTE - C.I.E.F.L. (EFLU), Hyderabad. p.2

2.   Introduction to Linguistics- 1988, P.G.C.T. E - C.I.E.F.L (EFLU)- Hyderabad. Lesson 3: A Thumbnail Sketch of The History of Western Linguistics. p.11

ii. Some Linguistic Aspects of English Language

Any language is primarily speech, writing comes later. You might have noticed that many tribal languages have no written script. Therefore, a language lives on and on in spoken form. Phonetics is the branch of linguistics that deals with speech sounds. English language has twenty-six alphabets but forty-four speech sounds. In phonology the basic speech sound is phoneme. But a phoneme has no independent meaning. The three phonological sounds: /b/ /u/ /k/ independently have no meaning. Whereas, together there is a word: book. That gives the meaning. Hence, a word has both i.e. signifier: the form and signified: the meaning. The word: book is a signifier i.e. a form (abstract). But the papers bound together in the book-form signifies meaning concretely. Similarly, words like: bat, mat, cat etc. are all for concrete forms of bat, mat, cat (material objects and animal). This being the case (a word has both a form and a meaning), can we take non-verbal symbols: like the red and green traffic lights as words? Because the red traffic light signifies or gives meaning to: stop and green for: go on. In the same way, online software symbols and social media icons (Facebook, Twitter, Instagram, and Google etc.), that are user friendly interfaces also signify or give meaning to the name of their companies. So, their user-interfaces, can they be called words (since they give meaning)? Likewise, mathematical symbols, when drawn like: a triangle, rectangle etc. give meaning, hence words? For clarity, even non-verbal symbols are also in linguistic parlance words. Because, they convey meaning. By seeing a series of curves, even a baby could make out that it is Wi-Fi! Now, there are certain other things of human behaviour that communicate or give meaning such as: facial expressions (angry, happy, irritated etc., type of feelings), the way we walk (rough, gentle, rash). Are they all words? No. Why? Because, to decipher from human behaviour or human facial expressions, we require some amount of psychology. For, it depends on how we perceive. Don't all emoji symbols in our cellular phones convey meaning? They clearly represent something. Are they considered as words? Yes, because they are fixed, unlike the transient human emotions.

Language Variations

Linguistics deals with many aspects of language. One of which is *Language Variations*. What are language variations? In a language, variations happen from time to time. Take any language, we are not speaking the eighteenth or nineteenth century kind. We speak the latest kind. Variations of language through time are called *diachronic variations*. The variations of language as they exist at a given point of time are called *synchronic variations*. These synchronic variations are of two kinds: *variations of dialect* and *variations of register*. Variations of dialect happen because of regions. In one language more than two, three dialects will be there depending on the regions people of the language community live. The fundamental difference between a dialect and a register is in the spoken and written forms. Dialects are variations in spoken language. Whereas, Registers are variations in written language.

Language and Dialect

The main limitation of traditional grammarians was, they did not recognise or wilfully ignored language variations viz. dialects and registers. Dialects come from the same language with slight regional variations. The proponents of structural approach also gave importance to dialect: varieties or variations in a language. Even in Telugu or Hindi different regions people speak different types of a variant of Telugu/Hindi. Dialects are different from languages. Languages like Telugu and Hindi are mutually exclusive, in the sense, of their intelligibility/ understanding. Bhojpuri and Malawi are two dialects of Hindi. In the same way, Andhra Pradesh and Telangana states' people speak two dialectal variations of Telugu language but are mutually intelligible i.e. would not be difficult to understand any of them for a Telugu-speaking person. Thus, the structural approach teaches not only structural patterns, but also vocabulary, situationally. That way, it is utilitarian. This structural approach has the backing of linguists and psycholinguists. This approach lasted for a long time in the methods of teaching English.

To extend further the definition of language and dialect, to get clarity, what the linguist E. Haugen said is important. As per E. Haugen, 'a dialect is a language that is excluded from polite society. It is, as Auguste Brun (1946) has pointed out, a language that 'did not succeed'. The "language" is more prestigious than the "dialect". Because of its wider functions it is likely to be embraced with reverence, a language loyalty that the dialects do not enjoy.'[1] In the language Telugu, there are two dialects: one is the Andhra dialect, the other is the Telangana dialect. Both these dialects come under the larger umbrella language: Telugu.

Registers in a language

The major variations come in a language in the form of registers. For instance, take any Indian language. The spoken language is different from the written. Even within one language: the legal/law, medical, journalistic, religious/scriptural languages are different. They are all called: 'Registers'. They should be written in that particular style. Sometimes we wonder, when we read a legal document (of property), is it the language I know or mine!

There is an anecdote to make clear what a Register is. It goes like this: In the 19th century an Englishman, Thomas Ward, went to China to learn Chinese. He went to a famous Chinese priest and expressed his desire to learn Chinese. "What sort of Chinese do you want to learn?" the priest asked him. "There is the Chinese of the sacred poetry, there is the Chinese of our ancients, and then there is the spoken Chinese, of which there are many dialects. Pray tell me, which Chinese, do you want to learn?"[2] The Englishman was confused and gave up the idea of learning Chinese. He did not realize one thing: even in English all these variations/varieties are there. In any language of relevance, all these registers are present. We switch from one register to the other as per the situation.

Writing Styles

Writing-styles differ depending on the person to whom we write and the context. We do not write in the same way, when writing to a friend or to the principal of school. Writing to a friend is informal and writing to the principal is formal. To use appropriate language for the appropriate person, comes under proper communication. Along with, here we keep in mind: formal or informal, official or personal languages. The advocates of the structural approach were greatly concerned about all these aspects. They recognised Registers: legal language that we read or write in legal documents: the Register of Law, similarly for scientific documents, the Register of science, the Register of journalism is found in newspapers, the Register of religion in religious scriptures, where often repetition of words and verses is done, so as to reinforce the prayer. So on and so forth for each field there is a specific kind of writing.

Langue and Parole

According to Ferdinand De Saussure; the pioneer of Linguistics, people that speak a particular language, have an abstract knowledge and skills of that language, for listening, speaking and also for the educated, reading and writing in that language. For instance, if I am a Telugu person, I understand what others in the same language community speak, when I listen to them. I also read and write (the common script shared by the Telugu community). De Saussure called this understanding of language principles or conventions of the language as *langue.*

Langue is the language system that is shared by all the members of a language speaking community.

What is a *parole* then? A *parole* is contrast to *langue*. *Parole* is the language used, when you are speaking, on a particular subject, on a platform (podium), say: *gender discrimination*. In that case, you use the language *specific* to that subject. If you are asked to write an essay on the subject, you use *specific* language pertaining to the topic given. That *specific* spoken or written language on the subject is called *parole*. Colloquially speaking, we all know that prisoners come out on parole. Suppose, a person is sentenced for three years or five years or life-long imprisonment, if on special conditions, he is permitted to be out of jail for a week or a month, we call, he is on *parole*. For, he has to be in jail normally, but to him, permission is given for a *specific* period to be out of jail. Hence, being in jail with fellow jailors, is the norm for him, being out on a specific period is *parole*. You use *specific* language on a *specific* topic in a lecture or for a piece of writing, that's called *parole*. But we do not use it (the specific language) all the while. So, *langue* is a set of rules and *parole* makes use of them for specific purposes of speaking and writing. Registers of language, come under *parole*. Because they are specific to the field.

Language in General

So, we now have *langue* and *parole*. Then, you may get a doubt, as to what a *language* is! Along with *langue* and *parole*, Saussure also defined a *language*. According to him, a *language* is the general faculty to express oneself with signs. As read earlier, *Signs* include: a *signifier* and *signified*. Of course, these are abstract mental constructs. When you hear someone talk, the sounds they send are *signifiers*, the meaning you construct is *signified*. If I say a 'blackboard' without pointing to any, you imagine many types and sizes of blackboards. Hence, the *sign*: blackboard is a physical object, the varied images produced by individuals are *signified* mental images or constructs. This faculty is common to natural human languages and not to artificial languages (computer languages). Programming languages JavaScript, C++, AI come under artificial languages.

In Saussure's finding: language is form, not substance. Sentences are structured according to an organized form. However, there are two types of underlined currents in this sentence- structuring. One is *syntagmatic* and the other is *paradigmatic*.

What is a syntagmatic relationship?

For instance, in a sentence:

E.g. *This is a fantastic way to answer your question.*

In the above sentence there is a relationship between the two words: *fantastic* and *way*. Similarly, between: *a* and *fantastic way*. The other parts are also connected in the same way. This relationship of adjoining words in the string is linear/sequential. Hence, it is syntagmatic.

Fantastic and *way* are two *syntagma* i.e. two linguistic units that enter into a syntagmatic (sequential) relationship. That means, the linguistic units (words) have a sequential relationship.

Now, what is a paradigmatic relationship?

The word *fantastic* (given in example above) has other forms viz.: *fantastically, fantasticalness, fantasticality*. And antonyms like: *un-fantastic.*

In the sentence (cited) the word: *way,* is a noun. In its plural form, it is - *ways.* So, therefore, within the word-level: synonyms, antonyms, other-forms of the same word, plurals of a word are all in paradigmatic relationships.

A *paradigm* means, a set of forms, all of which contain a particular element (especially in all words - inflected forms) based on a single stem or theme.

The *set of forms* mentioned, have an associative relationship. Hence, they are a paradigm. Their relationship is paradigmatic.

We have many sentence-types (interrogative, assertive, exclamatory, declarative etc.), there are also many clauses (finite-clause, non-finite-clause etc.), at word level: synonyms-antonyms, singular-plurals, words used in other forms are all paradigmatic, as they are associative (in conveying more or less same meaning). Hence, a language works on syntagmatic and paradigmatic associations of words, within the language.

Some Limitations of Structural Approach

Some of the limitations of structural approach are, merely by learning how to construct structures of English language, a student cannot speak or use the language as per the demands of the daily life situations. There are very many structures in English, which one to choose remains a question. If a person uses a wrong or inappropriate structure, his or her position becomes awkward. Moreover, structures only give a skeletal framework to a language. They do not adequately convey the meaning. They should be provided flesh and blood with expression and articulation. Teaching grammatical constructions at sentence-level may not help. Meaning of a sentence is not externally given, it is derived from the setting (where it is spoken), topic (about what), participant (whom) and the mood of the speaker. Such psychological and sociological factors affect language. To what extent can a teacher teach such a thing? Can they (psychological and sociological factors) be taught in a classroom? How? These questions are raised by researchers.

Here the Danish linguist Otto Jespersen's definition of language is important to note. He writes, 'The essence of language is human activity… activity on the part of one individual to make him understood by another, and activity on the part of the other to understand what is in the mind of the first … The speaker and hearer and their relations should never be lost sight of.'[3] Initially, the structural approach started with the backing of linguists like Bloomfield and psycholinguists like Skinner. Meanwhile, the Structural-Oral- Situational (S-O-S) approach came into prominence. In this approach vocabulary is presented through grades. Learning words of the language and syntax were given importance. This approach to teaching was later found to be inadequate to address the learning problems. In the structural approach, the learning process is a pure transfer of skills from the teacher to the students by the process of repetition or drilling. So, here the input is equal to the output. Hence the structural method, though easy to use, is a restricted one. For, it is inaccessible for the learner to use outside the classroom in the wider context. Suppose students are exposed to some patterns of sentences in a class or standard, they are limited to that. As a result, language thus learnt cannot become a tool for communication.

Language should not be a body of knowledge. That means, if you are learning 'grammar rules' of a language, you are gaining the 'knowledge' about the language, not the skills of using it. In the case of a grammar-centric and structural approach, what the students learn is about the language, not the language per se in use. When someone knows about something, it becomes knowledge. Learning grammar and learning structures come under knowledge. Therefore, language should not be a thing of knowledge. It has to be in 'use' and never be taught out of context. In communicative approach to the teaching of English, a learner is given time to process 'input' before expecting 'output'. In the structural approach, it has become customary to consider language as a series of building blocks known as patterns. So, language is treated as a 'form' rather than language as 'use'. This structural approach is based on an unproven premise. The approach based on structures or patterns did not deliver the desired result i.e., English as a language to communicate. Those who studied structure and grammar alone, were unable to express themselves in real life situations. As a result, many academics felt that communicative approach, in a way, coupled with structure and grammar in context or situation, eclectically, would serve the purpose.

Though learning structures of English is essential, that is not the be all and end all to communicate in the outside world. Hence, Chomsky's communicative approach gained currency. Primarily, his approach states that the human brain is holistic and it cannot be conditioned beyond a certain point. In the structural approach the human brain is conditioned or limited by the structures taught or laid down. The approach has not envisioned that the human brain could generate structures to suit the situation, as and when required. So, the fixation with structures is gone. The use of language in the day-to-day world obtained currency.

---

1.   E. Haugen, 'Dialect, language, nation', American Anthropologist, vol.68(1966), pp.922-35, Sociolinguistics, Selected Reading, edited by J.B. Pride and Janet Holmes, 1972, printed in Great Britain by Hazell Watson & Viney Ltd. pp. 100-103

2.   Introduction- Language and Linguistics 1988-P.G.C.T. E - C.I.E.F.L (EFLU), Hyderabad. p.18

3. N. Krishnaswamy 1971, An Introduction to Linguistics for Language Teachers, Somaiya Publications Pvt Ltd, 172, Naigaum Cross Road, Dadar, Bombay-14DD. p.122

iii. Leonard Bloomfield's Contribution to Linguistics

The American linguist, Leonard Bloomfield's significant contribution to the field of linguistics, is note-worthy. Bloomfield made linguistics "autonomous" i.e. an independent status, instead of being a branch like: anthropology, rhetoric or philosophy in the language. His analysis of linguistics was scientific.

Bloomfield had been under the influence of Behaviourist psychology i.e. to say the whole human behaviour in terms of response to stimuli. To Behaviourists, language is also a part of human behaviour. Behaviourism does not include things that are not directly observable or physically measurable from the domain of scientific enquiry. According to Bloomfield's theory of scientific enquiry: you could observe or measure statements about speech sounds and their distribution. They are empirically verifiable. You may get a doubt, as to how? In Language Lab you could get a graph of your acoustic sounds. So, it's verifiable. His obsession with scientific verification led to many revealing truths about language per se.

For instance, can you get the meaning or measure scientifically through a device (as is in the case of acoustic sounds), the meaning of the word: friendliness or happiness? No. For, they are abstract, they are our feelings, manifested in the form of some emotion but not scientifically measurable. The plain truth is, a sound can be recorded but the meaning cannot be recorded. For, meaning exists in the human mind. Bloomfield wanted his followers to pursue meaning until it became verifiable. So, for a long-time linguistics remained as: phonology, morphology and syntax. Then a later quest for 'meaning' was added. The branch of linguistics that deals with meaning is called semantics. It deals with the lexical meaning of the word and also the logical relationship of the word within the structure of a sentence. When you are writing some prose-text or a poem or a story or novel for publication or for a presentation in a seminar, you use different language devices, different styles to get an effect on your write-up. The branch of linguistics that deals with different styles of writing is known as Stylistics. For a person, knowing all grammatical rules of a language (here English) is to have the competence of language. If the same person could apply these rules and convey meaningfully what she wants to with others effectively, she is performing well. Hence, having the grammar rules of language is '*competence*' (in language) and articulating and conveying meaning through those rules in spoken or written form is '*performance*'. Both are important and interdependent. For, competence is something innate and performance is its outer manifestation.

Phonology, Morphology and Syntax – How they are related

Basically, linguistics deals with the structure of language. Language has a structure-dependence principle i.e. depends on grammatical structure. What are structures? What way are they particular to a language? Structures are dependent on grammar. In turn, grammar (of English) is dependent on morphology and syntax. Morphology is concerned with the structure of words; syntax is concerned with the structure of sentences. A morpheme is a meaningful unit in the grammatical system of language (sometimes single words are also morphemes). For e.g.: the words: photo and shop are two separate morphemes. Whereas, the word: *Photoshop* is a single morpheme, though it appears to contain two words: photo and shop. Photoshop is a minimal meaningful unit by itself. It is the proprietary name of a brand of computer software. Now coming to phonology, a phoneme is a smallest unit of sound. To be precise, a morpheme is the smallest unit of the grammatical system and a phoneme is the smallest unit of sound system. For e.g.: put … is a single morpheme but it has - three phonemes /p/- /u/ -/t/. In morphology, morphemes, though small particles, bring meaning. For e.g. glass is a morpheme (do not confuse a morpheme and a word are separate). It has /g/ /l/ /a: / /s/ -four phonemes. These phonemes are only speech sounds. They do not get any meaning separately. But morpheme, here: glass has an independent meaning.

Sometimes, to change a word to its plural, we add –s or –es, -ies, -ves (i.e. s-z-iz) etc., these are all again morphemes. In the same way, to make a word into past tense, we add –ed/-en, these are also morphemes. This morphological property comes from the *inflectional* and *derivational* properties of morphemes. Inflectional properties are related to different forms of the same word.

For e.g. girl- girls, car-cars, tomato-tomatoes, box-boxes etc.

The –s, -es are plural morphemes.

To go further, girl, car, tomato and box - used as examples, are also morphemes. They are mono-morphemic words.

Whereas, girls, cars, tomatoes, boxes have two morphemes, as we add the plural morpheme –s, -es (i.e. s-z-iz-0). Zero here applies to sheep, fish, etc; as the same words are plurals also.

Similarly, if you see past tense/past participle: look-looked, take-took by adding -ed, -en, (/t/, /d/) morphemes the word meaning of look and take do not change. Specially, nouns and verbs take inflectional morphemes.

In contrast, derivational morphemes used in prefixes and suffixes make a word a different kind of word.

For e.g. develop is a different word from development. The derivational suffix is; -ment.

In the same way negative prefixes e.g.: un- and in-, if added to words like: happy-unhappy, capable-incapable, the words (adjectives: happy and capable) change their meaning. That means words are derived from other words. So, they are derivational inflections.

Do the students need sufficient knowledge of the morphology and syntax of the language English? No. The teacher needs to and must be able to explain to students when needed. A student needs to have a passive knowledge of these grammatical aspects. The student's familiarity with the rules of word-formation, using prefixes like un-, in- etc. or suffixes like –tion, -ment etc. enable her to guess the meaning of new words. The student could also decode the sentence construction. The teacher in the class often asks students the antonyms and synonyms of words with different prefixes. In the same way, other-forms of words from a root-word. For a root-word like: beautiful, other forms are: beautifully, beautifulness. The other forms of words are tested contextually. Because, all prefixes and suffixes cannot be standardized to all words. Certain prefixes go with one kind of words, not with the others. Students need to know when to use what kind of prefix or suffix depending on words. Another advantage of knowing syntax and morphology is to know the categorisation of the word.

For instance: the word: manage - is a verb, by adding –ment, it becomes management - a noun so on and so forth. Take the word: dehumanization, it consists of morphemes: de-, human, -ize and –ation. The word: dislike consists of morphemes: dis- and like.

One may get a doubt: when morphemes are said to be minimal units which are meaningful, how can plural morphemes: -s, -es (/s/, iz) and past tense morpheme: /-t/, /d/, /-id/ and prefixes like: un- and suffixes like: -tion, -ment given above, do they have any meaning? When the very definition of a morpheme is a meaningful unit, the above mentioned should have meaning. Anyhow, they have their own meanings, though it is difficult to state clearly. Once you add a plural morpheme, it suggests or gives meaning of more than one. In the same way past tense morphemes indicate the meaning of something happened in the past i.e. not now. Prefix –un indicates negation. Suffix –tion changes the word to a noun, so therefore they are changing the meaning. Of course, we cannot fully rely on morphology to explain, for it is irregular. For instance, nowadays, schoolchildren, textbook, playground are all single words, unlike earlier there was word division i.e. leaving space between words.

After knowing about morphemes that are the minimal meaningful units, you may get a doubt as to what is a word in English. If a car, bus, girl, boy are all morphemes according to morphology, what are words? As a matter of fact, they are morphemes as well as words. Because they are all free-morphemes. To the contrary, -un, dis-, -ed etc. are not independent words. They are always attached to free morphemes: un-happy, dis-like, boy-boys, look-ed. Such morphemes (un-, dis-, -s, -ed types) are called bound morphemes. In the word: walking, walk is a free-morpheme but –ing is a bound morpheme. These bound morphemes are known as affixes (affix includes: prefix, infix, or suffix). Affixation is one kind of morphological structure of words. Another is by compounding, for e.g.: lockdown, hand sanitizer, mask up, mask drop etc. are compound words.

Syntax means how words are combined in a phrase or sentence. Since we cannot teach all of English, there is something called: selection of vocabulary and structure. Though there are millions of English words, vocabulary for school-texts is taken from frequently used words, the commonest words in speech and writing. Language learning involves not only lexical (vocabulary) learning but also structures: word order variation. These structures are particular to a language, meaning to say: there is variation in structure from language to language.

For e.g. Mr Ramesh is a doctor.

In this sentence, Mr Ramesh, is the - head of the sentence.

Head is followed by the complement - is a doctor.

Hence, English is a Head-First Language. English consistently puts head before complements. So do many Indian languages. The difference is English has a Subject-Verb-Object (SVO) pattern but most of the Indian languages have Subject- Object-Verb (SOV) pattern.

In questions, the initial wh-word is the head. For, its position is at the beginning of the sentence.

Grammar is all about principles that govern how to form and interpret words, phrases and sentences. In grammar there are content words: noun, verb, preposition, adjective and adverb. Whereas, number, gender, person, case etc. carry information about the grammatical function within the sentence. To explain further, pronouns like: 'he, she, and they' have no descriptive content, they are in the functional category.

For e.g.

Articles: a, an, the;

Pronouns: he, she, it, they, we;

Prepositions: in, on, under etc.,

Conjunctions: and, or, but etc.

Auxiliaries: is, are, has, have etc. and

Wh-words: What, which, when, how etc.

They are all frequently used but are taught as early as possible to a schoolchild.

Why are they taught early-on? Because they are structure words, while the nouns, adjectives, adverbs and verbs contribute to the content. There are too many content words. The number of meanings they convey make students of second language difficult to remember. Building up vocabulary is always a formidable task for second language learners (SLL). Nevertheless, they should be mindful of structure words. For, they are indispensable for one's use of English.

For instance, 'That girl *with* blue ribbons *is* carrying *a* basket full *of* vegetables.'

The words in italics: with, is, a, of - are also doing a function. Though they are little words, they are doing the bigger task of linking with the bigger words. So, they are structure words. Structure-words are not concrete.

The content words: ribbon, basket, vegetables (content words because they carry meaning), are linked by the structural words in a sentence or phrase.

The structural words are of great importance in the language. They are short and we rarely stress them while speaking. Hence, they go unnoticed. Many people concentrate on big words of vocabulary thinking that they are essential in learning English. However, learning these little structure words is more needed, without which those big vocabulary cannot be used. Do you see the difference between:

1. Going *to market* ... going *into market*.

2. I will go there *at six o'clock*... I will go there *by six o'clock*.
   If I say:

1. I want flags *in* 10 different places.

2. I want flags *with* 10 different places.

3. I want flags *of* 10 different places.

4. I want flags *for* 10 different places.

5. I want flags *on* 10 different places.

6. I want flags *from* 10 different places.

By the above examples, it is amply clear as to how structure words, though small, change the entire meaning of the sentence.

Generally, every English sentence carries at least one or two propositions. These are small words but do a heavy duty. Structural words cannot be taught in isolation. So, they are taught in phrases first viz. in front of, at the back of, a bunch of flowers, a pair of shoes etc. but teaching only phrases is not enough. They must be taught in sentences, so that they will be contextualized. Hence, in structural approach sentence patterns are taught. In primary school, English - sentence patterns are simple and formed around a verb, since the verb being the nucleus of the sentence. Later, in high school, the sentences are with many verbs. Further, subject-verb agreement and followed by tense-representation followed by how the verb takes object/complement etc. are taught to students in explicit grammar. In any case, there are many patterns of sentences with verbs.

In the English language, word-order is important: a stone house cannot be a house stone. The love of a mother cannot be the mother of love. These are word-orders in nouns. In adjectives when you are using more than one, for instance in a sentence: There are four tiny, little, black cats in the hole. Four, tiny, little, black (cats) - the arrangement of four adjectives is a pattern. A restricted one: you cannot say in a different manner like: little, tiny, black, four cats or in some other permutation.

Similarly, there is word-order for adverbs. For e.g. I like sweets very much. If I say: I very much like sweets - the meaning changes. In the same way, a sentence follows the pattern of Subject- Verb- Object/ Complement (SVO pattern). Finally, look at these sentences (this example is quite known in linguistic parlance):

1.   Sodium dissolves in water.

2.   A man dissolves in water.

Both 1&2 are structurally the same. That means they follow the same grammatically correct pattern of: subject-verb-object of the preposition. Yet, the first sentence is acceptable. The second is unacceptable. Because, going by meaning, a man cannot dissolve in water like sodium, the element. So, along with syntax, semantics (a branch of linguistics concerned with the study of meaning) plays a role. All that the students need to know is: to grasp the language patterns intuitively. For this, they need to get exposed to language by reading and speaking.

In skills like driving, swimming, cooking, there is something called intuition that guides. Constant practice gives this insightful intuitive thinking. Once the students are exposed to language, intuition plays a role. In the case of native speakers, intuition about grammar is in-built. It is part of native speaker's competence. Now, how to learn this grammar by a second language learner? Whether it is through formal teaching-learning or through subconscious acquisition? There are many hypotheses but no clear way out.

With regard to English grammar, Noam Chomsky in the 1990s proposed what is called: "minimalism". According to minimalism, grammar should make use of minimal theories and they should be as simple as possible. In this computer-internet-social media-age, people have become minimalist and follow the principle of economy in words while communicating. For e.g. the text messages. Once a student acquires the required grammatical structures, she must venture into language outside school curriculum to strengthen what is learnt and to improve. But that is not the case for non-natives of English. Because the student has no other experience of language, especially for the rural downtrodden, other than that is given in the textbook. Hence, English textbooks are prepared with a grammar section explained contextually. Even this context should also be related to students' experiential orbit. Since that experience is not available, the students depend on the teacher's explicit explanation of English grammar.

The drawbacks of Structural approach:

The structural syllabus deals with the 'form' of English language structure independent of 'use' (function). Hence, the needs of the learner to use the language is not taken care of. Therefore, the structural syllabus cannot be called student-oriented. Even if students use and practice structures, as given in the syllabus hundred percent, they cannot be put to use. Learning structure through substitution is based on the Behaviourist principle, where language learning is a matter of conditioning. The success of the student in learning the English language would not result in this syllabus, as it would not suffice to face real life situations.

Learning structures of a language means learning the internal system of the language. It would not cater to the needs of the students fully outside, i.e. externally. Teachers cannot evaluate the success of the lesson by the mere utterances made by the student in a class. The communicative approach to teaching involves student - participation. Hence, it is student-centred learning. For, communication cannot take place if the teacher speaks alone all the time. Student-centric learning demands the design of the syllabus in that orientation of involving the students in the classroom. Students are supposed to learn on their own rather than depending on the teacher to do it entirely. Nonetheless, even while students are pursuing to do the tasks on their own, they need the teacher's monitoring and guidance. The presence of the teacher in the classroom and her watch is much needed. Because for the teaching learning to take place, a teacher is as much responsible as the students. Her movement in the class, in between rows, assisting the students while needed, when they are doing the task, is vital.

Even in the structure-based syllabus, student-involvement and participation is necessary. But it was restricted. Students need to utter a single word or structure constantly in the class like that of a drill or substitution-table from the beginning to the end. A student-oriented English lesson would be the one, where students do not need to utter a single word or structure constantly in the class. The class is only meant for speed-reading or listening and writing activities. Contrast this with the student-oriented communicative approach. In communicative approach, students actively participate and full-control is given to them. Moreover, a language evolves with meaning not with structure.

iv. Communicative Approach

The communicative approach is based on the cognitivist principle, according to which language learners possess some kind of data-processing mechanism. With this, she processes the input data to derive on her own accord system of language rules. This gives scope for the learner to produce other sentences. The students' involvement in communicative activities requires listening, speaking, reading and writing and thinking too while doing the same. Students' performance would be lively. In any performance there are actors and a director. If we consider the students to be actors and the teacher the director, the teacher needs all skills. Sometimes, in higher classes, students themselves could become actors and directors, while writing and playing small skits.

Then the paradigm-shift has taken place from structural approach to communicative approach to the teaching of English. Basically, the shift was for the language class to be utilitarian. It has to cater to the future needs of the students, who have to use it in the world, where required. Communication is, quintessentially, interaction between individuals. In this approach, students are trained to think and act on their own in the target language. Learning objectively, what the text says (that maybe or may not be remembered and applied by the students in their life), is supposedly futile.

'Use' is the key-word in any communicative language. 'Use' includes: conversation, communication, context and appropriateness. In communicative approach, language is learnt entirely for its practical benefits. This approach creates situations to use the language. In a situation thus created, the student is needed to talk. In a way, it is problem-solving. This way, language is taught in a natural, meaningful and realistic way. Structural-patterns are used situationally with an appropriate language. The earlier approaches did not yield satisfactory results in India. Hence, switching on to the communicative approach of teaching became imminent.

Noam Chomsky, the renowned linguist coined the term: LAD i.e., Language Acquisition Device. All humans are born with an in-built clockwork to learn a language. Even a months-old baby starts uttering some syllables, small words at a certain point of time. Otherwise, parents get worried. Chomsky says a child learns the language like learning to walk. This is because of the internal drive of the child. Children are born inherently with a language acquisition device (LAD). Along with, to acquire and communicate in a language, cognitive ability (connected with mental process or understanding) plays a role. In communicative approach, importance is given to the learner i.e., learner-centred. In learner-centred teaching learners should put in effort. The teacher's role is only that of a facilitator. To facilitate (to take place) the language learning, the teacher should have command over the language and be equipped with the linguistic tools, methods and material to guide the students, as and when necessary. To take this communicative approach forward, a teacher needs to be more skilful. After all, the teacher's aim should be to make the student autonomous i.e. independent of the teacher. Once the student knows how to read, understand, speak and write on his own in English, she does not need an English teacher. That is what student autonomy is all about. Being on her own in learning and gaining knowledge through language, she is likely to surpass the teacher. Hence, teachers need to aim at making students independent-learners.

Is the communicative approach of teaching English perfect? Let's see the inherent troubles. Communicative approach touches upon the functional aspects of language. 'Forms' that are based on structure or grammar of language, are subservient to the 'use' of language, as vehicles for meaning. For e.g.; May I come in, please? is a question according to its 'form' or structure. But the function or in 'use', it is serving the purpose of: seeking permission. Hence, the structure is subservient to the function it is serving.

Conclusively, structure is form-focussed and communication is function or meaning-focussed. The problem with the communicative method of teaching English is: there are no universally accepted (or agreed) and adequate descriptions of 'functions' of language. For instance, for exchanging greetings, giving instructions, making requests, making suggestions for all these and umpteen number of other functional aspects, there are more than one way to do this. All cannot be taught; all cannot be exposed to a student. Moreover, while teaching in communicative approach, a teacher faces a problem of how to teach a list of discrete 'functions', in the similar way, how she has felt while teaching discrete 'structures' in the structural approach.

In effect, the questions are: how many structures or forms can a teacher provide a student to learn in structural syllabus? Similarly, how many functions can a child learn to communicate effectively, in communicative syllabus? So, it is 'common sense' of a teacher, which drives her to conclude, structure is considered necessary, but not a sufficient component in a second or foreign language syllabus.

Another vital point to be discussed is: grammar-based and the structural way of syllabus, demands for the conscious effort of concentration, on the part of students for learning. In contrast, in the communicative approach, "acquisition" of language is a subconscious process. In it, human beings (since, it is language acquisition process 'human beings' are referred to. It includes students of language-learning also) abstract, process and organize relevant data from the linguistic environment and store it in memory ready for use and retrieval.

Learning, as a voluntary and conscious effort by an individual can be monitored and corrected. That takes place in the structural approach. Whereas, in functional approach, acquisition of language is an involuntary process and is beyond control or monitoring and is not subject to rationality. One may doubt rationality. In the structural method, it is rule-governed. The violation of the rule or logic behind the rule, could be found-fault with. This cannot be applied to the acquisition process, as it depends on the mental make-up of the child. The same explanation of a lesson, different students grasp in different ways. And the teacher has no control on their minds, as they are left free to infer. Often, teachers get baffled, while correcting the answer-sheets of students, with different interpretations of what the teacher taught rather than the proper one.

Krashen (1985) input-hypothesis, finds fault with all the above approaches. Specially, with regard to the communicative approach to teaching of English, which is the most followed pedagogic approach in India, Krashen (in one of his webinars during the pandemic years) says, 'Nobody knows what communicative approach is. Therefore it should not be used anymore. For many people it is "talking right away"'. Many ESL teachers would agree with what he said. For students of second language English, it is difficult to speak in English to communicate. Then, how can the "communication" take place? Krashen views, 'asking ESL learners to talk straight away in English', is wrong. This approach is used to force people to talk before they are ready for it. In that case, how could they call it communicative approach, he questions. Next, their mistakes in grammar and other aspects of pronunciation are not corrected in this approach. This approach could be used as a part of 'comprehensible input' methodology.

Krashen brushed aside even Immersion methodology to learn a language by going to the native country of the language to learn. Unless the language is comprehensible, it cannot be learnt. He suggests reading stories and novels as the best way to learn the language. The reading material should be interesting and compelling to read. To him a language class has to begin with a story.[1]

As far as language is concerned (any language not only English), acquisition of the language is easily possible, when the environment is sufficiently rich with data. Of course, as per Krashen the data or input should be comprehensible. Even if we provide the comprehensible (though not possible, one-set for all learners) to measure what is acquired, it is quite difficult, as acquisition is self-regulated (not by the teacher's external force or rule-bound) mechanism. Moreover, certain items are easily acquired by certain learners only. And not by others. Some items are even resistant to learning. These (resistant items) vary from learner to learner. That the teacher needs to identify. To sum up: the ESL students are provided with a restricted variety of linguistic contexts … very few role-relationships and a limited number of speech functions in English, since English is their second or third language. So, therefore, with that limited in-put to attain fluency in language is difficult.

Questions to ponder over

Do we need all learners to develop excellent communication in English in India? Is the communicative approach followed in the West i.e. in the English-speaking countries to be followed in India? When acquiring a second language, the immigrant's population in the U.S. is surrounded by English every day. This facilitates learning in the 'Natural Method'. While living in India, to absolutely learn English and learn it well, is not possible. The immigrant children in the U.S.A and U.K. learn English as a second language. They have a very strong enabling learning environment. It is compulsory for them to know English to survive in that country. In India, it is possible to survive without English. It is not an imperative. In an English-speaking country, English language ability is far more internalized and solidified because people use it every day in all circumstances. That atmosphere is not found for Indian students. Be it in any of our offices or schools, the local language dominates. Our state-offices work without any need to use English. Only official files are moved, sometimes, with some amount of English. Not having much English is not a serious disadvantage in India.

1.   https://youtu.be/uLBMtL4JuRM (1.15.57 to 1.16.31)

v. Drawbacks Of Communicative Approach

As stated earlier, in the Communicative approach the language "acquisition" by the student is not measurable or quantifiable, as acquisition itself is something cognitive. Earlier, structuralism exponent Bloomfield also sought for every aspect of language learning to be scientific and measurable. Since in communicative approach language acquisition is not measurable, teachers hold to the traditional model of teacher-centric teaching. The reasons being:

1. What if they (the teachers) will lose the hold on students?

2. What if the 'acquisition' of language has not taken place in some students as desired?

3. What if the 'acquisition' does not reflect in answering the examination?

4. What if that unseen 'acquisition' that has no measurable yardstick, has happened or not, to the level of expected outcomes?

Acquisition of language may help in the future for students in life. Researchers suggest that there is a 'silent period' in exhibiting what is acquired at students' subconscious level. Yet, the teacher in the context has her own apprehensions of the process. In contrast to "acquisition of language", Alan Maley views 'learning a language' is better. It is measurable and quantifiable to an extent. He writes, 'Learning (of a language) is characterized by the need for a conscious effort of concentration on what is being learned…It is subject to a monitor mechanism---that is, a kind of psychological censor, which vets all items before they are uttered, and corrects them if it detects an error.'[1]

The above argument of Maley's learning-analysis is likely to be appreciated by many in the teaching community. For, all teachers are attuned to this kind of thinking. Teachers in the activity/ task-based – method, need to let loose children to do the activities on their own. A conscientious teacher on one-side, feels that she is not doing her duty by not teaching lessons conventionally. She would become doubtful of learning to take place with student-to-student intervention (intervention is to become involved in a situation in order to improve). Her job here (in cognitive method) is only to provide conditions for acquisition to happen. To this (for acquisition to happen), there is a need to monitor students while doing activities by: seeing, observing and by guiding where it is needed. The learners themselves have to learn.

Further, going back to the credit of text-analysis-based syllabus, the products of that syllabus turned out to become the erudite scholars most of the time. The literary values of the text had a deep impact on the generation. Moreover, the syllabus was rich in vocabulary. Students developed a flair for the English language. Some pursue higher studies in English literature, though not all. The communicative syllabus and modern method of teaching is restricted in this aspect.

1. Alan Maley, New lamps for old: realism and surrealism in foreign language teaching, *ELT Journal,* Volume 37, Issue 4, October 1983, pp. 295-303, https://doi.org/10.1093/elt/37.4.295

vi. Student-centric learning

The student-centric learning is the aspirational goal of the education system. Of all the methods or approaches followed, the most student-centric approach is the constructivist approach. In the constructivist approach, students are co-constructors of knowledge along with the teacher. They involve, as active participants, along with the teacher in the classroom. Their learning outcomes result from their actions of negotiation with their peers in group-work, pair-work and role-play kind of collaborative activities. By working so (with their peers), they shed inhibitions and language barriers to clarify their doubts. The only thing the teacher has to take care of is: to involve students in activities and work that is relatable to their experiential orbit. And also ensure the support in the areas of difficulty by the teacher's active presence. However, many teachers in the field opine that this student-centric approach is more chaotic and not disciplined like in the teacher-centred method. Moreover, whether all the students understood the lesson or could answer in the examination is questionable.

The term student-centred or student-centric (sometimes called child-centered) learning/education has become widely accepted ... not well defined and, arguably, in many countries around the world, more aspired than actually practiced.'[1] writes William Bill Atweh in his paper on 'Beyond Student Centered Learning towards Educative Pedagogies,'. By writing so, he was not asking for going back to traditional forms of teaching and learning. He was just elaborating how crucial the teacher's role is in educational reform. In a way, he mentioned in his paper on the limitations of child-centric learning. Interestingly, he refers to the contributions of many theorists of the past century such as John Dewey, Jean Piaget, Lev Vygotsky and Carl Rogers, who have challenged our thinking about how learning occurs in children and have led to theories and practices known as constructivism. Constructivism highlights the active role of students in learning. So, therefore it is incorporated in educational planning and execution.

He further states, these theories: like that of constructivism, contain some common elements. Could you guess what those common elements are? All these theories, he points out that the teacher's teaching is not equal to that of the students' learning. That is, what the students learn is not the same as what the teacher attempts to teach. Meaning to say, what the teacher gives as input will not be the same as students' output. Their understanding depends, sometimes, on their cognitive perception. Often teachers find fault with students for their lack of understanding. They attribute this to students' laziness, absent-mindedness, disinterestedness in the subject etc.; but it is not so.

The student-centric, activity- based classes take the teacher away from centre-stage. For a long time, teacher- hegemony prevailed in the classrooms. In the student-centric method, teachers feel insecure about losing control over students, after playing a major role all these days. Teachers all the while used to prepare for the class to dominate, by giving their version of the lesson to be understood. In student-centric classes, students do activity-based tasks, so that involuntarily, without any threat to their self-esteem, they learn language in participation with their peer-group.

Atweh poses some problems finally, they still remain as problems in the education field and the constructivist-approach. This is mainly pertaining to teachers in the field. He writes, The challenge in education should be how to engage teachers in practices that engage students ... the very concept of 'centred' is problematic since it implies that other factors are peripheral and hence it fails to deal with the complex phenomenon of educating students.'[2]

On the whole, in the process-oriented- student-centric constructive learning, the teachers' job is lively, participatory and rewarding, when a student comes out with desired outcome by his own effort. Whatever students acquire by their own cognitive abilities is everlasting than what a teacher makes them learn. After all, the whole effort of teaching the language is to make them autonomous learners. A teacher should progressively become irrelevant for the language learner. How does this happen? Only when the student is capable of reading a text on her own and comprehending it. For such a student, there is no looking back. No need for props from the language teacher. Towards that end, the teacher should equip students with all required skills.

1. Bill Atweh1 (b.atweh@curtin.edu.au) Science and Mathematics Education Centre Curtin University of Technology, Australia, "Beyond Student Centred Learning towards Educative Pedagogies", ICER 2011: Learning Community for Sustainable Development: September 9-10, 2011, KKU, Thailand. pingpdf.com_download-icer-2011-proceedings-revised-full-paper.pdf p.21

2. Ibid p.22

vii. Some Other Time-tested Methods/Approaches

The **Constructivist Approach** is the most followed approach in teaching pedagogy. When teaching is for construction of knowledge, learning is a process of that construction of knowledge. Connecting new ideas to the existing ideas on the basis of materials and activities presented to students constructivism is done. The structuring and restructuring of ideas are essential features, as the learners' progress in learning. The very meaning of constructing is learning. The constructivist approach provides strategies for promoting by all. 'Intelligent guessing'---is a valid pedagogical tool in this approach. Schools must provide opportunities for students to question, enquire, debate, reflect and arrive at concepts to create new ideas. In the constructivist approach, student participation is much needed. A student is a co-constructor of knowledge along with the teacher. Learning is a process of constructing. According to this theory, 'knowledge cannot be instructed by a teacher, it can only be constructed by a learner.' Constructivism takes a cognitive approach to teaching.

There is another approach called the **Natural Approach**. This approach consists of lexical (vocabulary) items, structures and messages (communication containing information: news, advice, request etc.). To understand the vocabulary by knowing and to produce them in an organized and interpretative way is critical to this method.

In Kerala, Andhra Pradesh and Telangana states, the textbooks published by state boards follow: **Discourse Oriented Pedagogy**. This approach critiques fragmentary structures and skill-based approaches viz. LSRW in communicative approach to English language teaching. English could be meaningfully learnt through discourse i.e. a mode of communication of certain ideas meaningfully conveyed in a certain way situationally. A paragraph in the reading passage is also a discourse. Because teachers make a big reading passage into meaningful chunks for students to read, understand and discuss. For e.g. narratives, rhymes, conversations, descriptions etc. all come under discourses. Discourse oriented pedagogy proceeds from whole to part but some of the other approaches focus from part to whole. In discourse-oriented pedagogy focus is on process but not on the product. This approach critiques fragmentary (structures) and skill-based approaches to English language teaching. English could be meaningfully learnt through discourse i.e. a mode of communication of certain ideas meaningfully conveyed in a certain way situationally.

There is also **task-based learning**. Dr N.S. Prabhu is one of the pioneers in the development of task-based learning and the communicative teaching of language through his work on the Bangalore Project ... the project has since become one of the bases of current language learning theory and practice... Prabhu advocated problem-solving and task-based programme for the acquisition of second language.[1]

All the teachers are aware of **presentation, practice, production (PPP) method** of lesson planning. It is the most used way of writing the lesson plan i.e. teachers introduce new vocabulary and grammatical structures, then they make students practice and produce sentences with it. This practice was more prevalent in the transition period of situational language teaching and communicative language teaching methods. Communicative language teaching emphasized the importance of free communicative activities, whereas in PPP the activities are controlled productions. '**Task-based language teaching (TBLT)** was developed as an alternative to traditional methods such as grammar translation, the **Audiolingual Method or present–practice–produce (PPP)**. It has received increasing support from a number of Second Language Acquisition (SLA) researchers. 'Task-based language teaching aims to develop learners' communicative competence by engaging them in meaning-focused communication through the performance of tasks'.[2]

The New Education Policy (NEP) 2020 is encouraging a **multilingual approach** in the English classroom teaching. Though multilingualism has been emphasized way back in educational policies, it has been now realized. India is a multilingual country. This multilingualism should be taken as an advantage. Hence, a multilingual approach to the teaching of English has come to the forefront. Multilingualism, which is constitutive of the identity of a child and a typical feature of the Indian linguistic landscape, must be used as a resource, classroom strategy and a goal by a creative language teacher. This is not only the best use of a resource readily available, but also a way of ensuring that every child feels secure and accepted, and no one is left behind on account of his/her linguistic background in the English class to participate in all activities.

All the above teaching- methods and approaches come under English teaching pedagogy, which all English teachers have studied to a greater or lesser extent during their Bachelor of Education (B.Ed.) Degree. **Pedagogy** is a broader term formed by an educator's teaching beliefs. Teaching pedagogy is important because what the teacher teaches through an approach or method would affect the learners. Here, only some concerns are raised about those methods and approaches. Doubts are expressed. Frequently, in the in-service English teachers' training programmes (otherwise known as: the Continuous Professional Development -CPD- programs) the academic scholars would remind that learning a language should be a discovery type i.e. a creative theory. Instead of treating the language as a body of knowledge, it should be treated as a means for getting things done. Too often teachers lose sight of the fact that only learners can learn, teachers cannot learn for them. Hence, teachers should organize activities which favour fluency more than accuracy in a language class. Techniques like role-play of skits/ dramas, two-minute talks on any topic of interest, assigned group-work, debates, elocution etc. is useful.

The judicious use of structural and communicative approaches can be used to attain this goal.' However, on the ground the reality is different. When teachers are held responsible for the students' performance in the examination, teachers' role and attitude will always be teaching for the examination to save their skin.

Yet, a section of teachers follows what has been taught in the CPDs, as they also know that the means are as important as the ends.

Finally, one might get a doubt, as to what is the distinction between: a method and an approach. A method is one that follows techniques and procedures of teaching language, whereas an approach is a set of general principles on how to go about to teach a language. So, the distinction is somewhat blurred. A teacher of English could apply her choice of techniques to suit the general principles of teaching.

It is pertinent to remind here, what the research paper on: "The Best Method to Teach English Language," says. It was published in the ELK Asia Pacific Journal, March 2015. The study was done by two researchers. At the end of their paper, they write, 'In conclusion, the study says a range of approaches is required to improve English proficiency in India, and no single method will help.'[3] This is how in CPD programs, often English teachers are advised.

1. "The teacher's sense of plausibility" by Alan Maley, doi: 10.29366/2018 tlc.2.1.2, Training Language and Culture, Volume 2 Issue 1, 2018, *The act of teaching and learning is not scientific but highly individual and personal to both learners and teachers'* doi: 10.29366/2018 tlc.2.1.2, rudn.tlcjournal.org

2. Task-based language teaching, Exploring Language Pedagogy through Second Language Acquisition Research, Rod Ellis and Natsuko Shintani, Routledge Introductions to Applied Linguistics, *Exploring Language Pedagogy through Second Language Acquisition Research - (2014).pdf) p.135

3. Dr. T. Jeevan Kumar and Mrs G. Sailaja, ELK Asia Pacific Journal, March 2015, https://www.researchgate.net/publication/282974160 p.3

Chapter- 3

Different Syllabuses and Modes of Teaching

Teachers often keep syllabus completion in mind. They make lesson-planning as per the syllabus to be completed in that month. However, most often teachers get a doubt: what is it called a syllabus? and what is it called a curriculum? The contents of a curriculum are known as syllabus. Whereas curriculum is an aggregate of course to study. Content-based syllabus was followed earlier in the 1960s and 70s. Later academic realization was that, that it would not lead to language use i.e. language-communication. Hence, task-based learning, communicative-approach have come into place. Let us see what is content-based syllabus and what way it does not help communication.

i. Content-Based Syllabus

Years ago i.e., during the grammar-translation method period, the text-analysis-based syllabus was taught. According to that syllabus, the teacher analysed and explained the text given in order to make students comprehend. This is teacher-centred learning. The teacher had a major role to make students understand. The students were almost passive listeners. The text was pre-determined on its literary and content value to be grasped by students. The content was simplified to explain the level of students by the teacher. The text did not keep in view the needs of the students. But the values in the text were profound and the wisdom of it was everlasting. That could be the reason, as to why old people studied in that generation talk of value-based education. Even now, textbook material is prepared based on certain principles or values, although different from the old. Textbooks of the present are developed with objectives to be inculcated in schoolchildren are: spirit of adventure, culture of the country and food, humour in life, self-discipline, punctuality, empathy on the old, weak and socially deprived, human relations, spirit to fight against superstitions in the society, love for science, environment and sports.

On the other hand, when it comes to reading the text and vocabulary, the difficulty in reading is generational. Interestingly, in 1963 Prof Randolph Quirk (the then Professor of English at the University of London) wrote a report on English teaching in India. The brief excerpt from the report that was made more than sixty-years ago, still resonates to an extent in India, showing the incapacity of reading English text by some students. Pointing to the defect in syllabus he then writes, 'Students who are scarcely able to read a restricted vocabulary text are expected to study a Shakespeare play, some of Jane Austin at her subtlest, some of Pickwick papers at their most colloquial ... and sporadic poems from the seventeenth to the nineteenth century.'[1]

Those rich content-based teaching materials were used in undergraduate classes then. Therefore the changes that have taken place in the syllabus now are gradual and well thought out. The introduction of gradation in vocabulary, grammatical structures, communicative and utilitarian language are as a result of recognising the fact that old methods of teaching are of no use in the modern day-to-day world. Hence, for higher classes: issues relating to adolescence, science and technology, the nation-diversity (socio-cultural, religious and ethnic, as well as linguistic), heritage (myths/legends/folktales), self, family, home, friends and pets, neighbourhood and community at large, the world and India's neighbours, peace and harmony, travel and tourism, mass media, art and culture, health and reproductive health are all topics that deal with the here and now. In the earlier content-based syllabus, this specificity to cover all aspects of life was not overtly given importance to incorporate in the syllabus.

1. Lesson 2, The Art of Material Production-A Review by ML Tickoo and BN Kaul, MATERIALS FOR TEACHING OF ENGLISH- C.I.E.F.L. p.7

ii. How Should Second Language Teaching Be?

English teachers, especially that are teaching in mother-tongue or local-medium schools, often tend to teach English subject in students' mother tongue or local language i.e. L1. That way of teaching is easier than to painfully make students understand English-to-English. Academicians, who are not day-to-day regular teachers, say many theories for teachers on how to go about in their classes when teaching.

Let us talk about this statement given.

Teaching a second language can never be the same as 'teaching' a first language. A learner who has learned one language knows a lot about human languages. He has built a universal grammar and this helps him in learning other languages. Only significant differences in the other languages are to be learnt.'[1]

It is not as simple as stated, especially in the case of English, the second language. Perhaps, it is true with adults that are keen on learning another language. People that voluntarily wish to learn another language, make an effort to compare and contrast with their first language (L1). In the case of English learners at school level, English is a compulsory subject. It is not a voluntary choice or leisurely activity to learn the English language by differentiating rules that are followed in L1. Moreover, their L1, as it fulfils all their needs, does not allow the other language i.e. English to flourish in the Indian environment.

The proposition, that is: 'student has built a universal grammar and this helps him in learning other languages' would not work in the case of schoolchildren because they learn the second language in a conditioned environment. Apart from that, the English grammar is distinct. Yet, these statements come from academicians. By making clear the subtle differences between the L1, most often their mother tongue, and the second language English, would not automatically make them acquire L2 i.e., the English language. Sometimes, at best, it clears some of the grammatical concepts. A student in a class is not in an exclusive English club or an English learning institute. He has umpteen other complex concepts to learn in other subjects. The limited attention of forty-five minutes in a class, would not deliver the language goals.

Stephen Krashen's theories on language learning

Stephen Krashen, the renowned linguist is known for his theories of learning a language i.e. Second Language - L2. Krashen summarizes his basic proposition in terms of a single claim: 'people acquire second languages only if they obtain "comprehensible input" and if their "affective filters" are low enough to let the input in'[2]. Here, it is pertinent to know the affective filter hypothesis of Krashen for all English teachers.

'The **Affective Filter** hypothesis embodies Krashen's view that a number of 'affective variables' play a facilitative, but non-causal, role in second language acquisition. These variables include: motivation, self-confidence, anxiety and personality traits. Krashen claims that learners with high motivation, self-confidence, a good self-image, a low level of anxiety and extroversion are better equipped for success in second language acquisition. Low motivation, low self-esteem, anxiety, introversion and inhibition can raise the affective filter and form a 'mental block' that prevents comprehensible input from being used for acquisition. In other words, when the filter is 'up' it impedes language acquisition. On the other hand, positive affect is necessary, but not sufficient on its own, for acquisition to take place.'

To Krashen "comprehensible input" means the input that is understandable. To this he proposes free-reading i.e., to read story-books, comics and novels that are easily understandable to the learner. That would enable a learner, grasp the language easily. To him, these books should also be self-selected. According to Krashen, if a person selects on her own, she would definitely read the books thus selected. "Comprehensible input" is always emphasized by Krashen. For, a child cannot read and understand adult-books. Moreover, that which is not understandable is uninteresting to read. If one were to understand what they would read, they need to understand the words/vocabulary used in what they read to an extent and also the background knowledge of the text. For instance, if a text has heavy historical and political undertones, many adult readers also would not comprehend. Hence, they would not go any further to read it.

This interest in reading develops over a period with the encouragement of parents and also teachers to an extent. Not all schoolchildren have it. Because, reading requires a lot of effort on the part of the learner to do by himself or herself. This has to be acquired rather than something taught in the class. This raises the question: how many students would spare their time to read although it is useful to them? In this digital-age, children have moved on to viewing pictorial stories on screen or listening to rather than solitary reading. Do you accept that reading and understanding what is read alone would lead to a language learning? Then what about the other skills of listening, speaking and writing? Are they not required to acquire the English language? Does your speaking skill enhance by reading alone? Is your writing-skill dependent only on extra reading material? Yes, to a great extent. But speaking and writing are productive skills. That is, you produce what you accumulate (as vocabulary and structure) by reading, isn't it? Yes, the input is reading, the output is speaking and writing. Moreover, the input of reading enhances the productive skills. No doubt about it. On the other hand, the output of speaking and writing are also helpful in language promotion and acquisition. How? Go back and reflect. While speaking, especially the L2 learners, sometimes get a doubt as to whether they are using the appropriate word or phrase or idiom in their speech. In the same way, while writing an examination or an essay or any piece of writing, learners of L2 often doubt their usage. So what do learners do? They refer to some dictionary or thesaurus or clarify things from their teacher or from an expert in the language. Speaking and writing, though productive skills, would give scope to testing yourself. By referring and clarifying, you gain knowledge.

For all that, there is no direct role for "output" in Krashen's theory. To Krashen, the ability to speak in an L2 develops only as a result of the acquisition that takes place through "comprehensible input" in reading. Krashen also talked about: "The Affective Filter Hypothesis". According to that Krashen says: for 'acquisition (of the language)' to take place, learners need to be 'open' to input; if learners are unmotivated, lacking in self-confidence or anxious, input, even if comprehensible, does not reach the learner's language acquisition device.[3] What does 'open to input' means? Open to input means a child should be free i.e. with no fear. A learner should have a non-threatening environment to learn. No forcible imposition. The fear of a teacher causes anxiety. Krashen also wanted a learner to be motivated, confident and free from anxiety in learning L2.

The opposite of which: lack of motivation or self- confidence and anxiety are the "affective filters" that hamper the acquisition or learning of language according to him. Krashen wanted the "affective filters" bar to be very low in the English language classroom.[4]

Most learners in Indian schools routinely learn English, as it is in the curriculum along with other subjects compulsorily to be learnt. Like in learners' mother-tongue, the learner has to obtain thirty-five marks to pass to the next class even in English. That means on equal footing with that of the student's mother tongue. If he fails in English, he needs to repeat the examination. If a student has failed in securing a pass mark, after attending the whole year, after the thorough coaching by the teacher, can she or he by privately appearing for supplementary exams, pass the same? There was a proposal in the National Curriculum Framework (NCF 2005), which is appropriate to mention here. NCF 2005 on Language Education says specially about English language: 'Language evaluation need not be tied to "achievement" with respect to particular syllabi…Evaluation is to be made an enabling factor for learning rather than an impediment… A student may be allowed to "pass without English" if an alternative route for English certification (and therefore instruction) can be provided outside the regular school curriculum.'[5] That being clarified, the question arises on the accountability of English teachers with no feedback from Board examinations. How could English teachers be bereft of accountability, when other languages' teachers and the subject teachers are? The Board examinations are an acid-test for both teachers and pupils. So, minimum qualifying marks for students and maximum class average in the English subject should be set i.e. on par with the other subjects.

Jespersen views on acquisition of English language

Jespersen (the Danish linguist) proposed that the "acquisition of English language" would hardly apply to English as a second or third language. Jespersen's quote on language acquisition: 'An infant is not taught the grammatical rule that the subject is placed first, or the indirect object regularly precedes the direct; and yet, … he will abstract some notion of their structure … in framing sentences of his own.'[6] Jespersen's basic assumption is correct to the extent that language acquisition has to take place unconsciously. Equally true is his other statement that it would not apply to English as a second language.

Jespersen's other statement, 'from the innumerable sentences heard and understood, definite enough to guide him in framing sentences of his own,'[7] may not apply to the English second language learners (SLL) in India. The learner has neither the privilege of hearing innumerable sentences nor has the latently stored target language to frame sentences of his own. Yet this system of language acquisition continues in the schools. The grammatical approach of teaching English as a second language is a failed approach. Grammar is touched situationally in the structural approach and communicatively in the communicative approach. To talk about the language, the English teachers make an effort to teach grammar consciously at times, which is desirable. By overtly teaching grammar, as is done in the grammatical approach to learning the language, the conscious effort of a child and learning English as a subject to be learnt with effort put in, makes it (English) intimidating.

Noam Chomsky-Language acquisition-specific to humans

The "innateness hypothesis" of Noam Chomsky: 'language acquisition process is innate to human beings', is widely accepted. For our pet animals, however much time they spend with us and hear us speaking, they cannot talk our language. Therefore, language is a species-specific ability of humans. For language acquisition i.e. one's mother-tongue or the surrounding native language, one need not have to have 'intelligence'. Do you call a child picking up language around intelligent? No. All children do so. Even a stupid or dullest child would also pick up the language around. Chomsky, to support his "innateness hypothesis", goes on to say that language acquisition is a totally subconscious and involuntary activity. Involuntary because you do not choose or wish to learn native L1 language, like how to choose to play cricket or not. The native/mother tongue language is somewhat unguided i.e. parents do not teach the child how to talk. Of course, there will be immediate correction, if the child says something wrong. Children learning their mother tongue/native language is genetically an in-built mechanism.

Chomsky says for years together the basic conundrum faced by the study of language has been … there are different conditions to satisfy to learn a language. They are all conflicting. One of the conditions to satisfy is: it has to account for how children acquire the language. The study of language acquisition by two-three years old children provides essential properties of language. From what they exhibit, there is rich enough data available for language acquisition theory. And with that knowledge of language evolved within a brief period in evolutionary terms. Notwithstanding, this child's innate capacity for acquisition of language, would it apply to second or third language learning or acquisition, is the question? There are individual differences. For, majority of people, if they pass the age of puberty, difficulty of acquiring a second language happens. The small children have no such problem. The child can learn five, six languages simultaneously without knowing they are different languages. They assume they are different ways to speak to people. We do this at some level. When we get to a certain age i.e. after puberty it becomes much more difficult. That's called the critical *period* by Chomsky. At that age we have a fixed-faculty of language. Hence, it is more difficult to acquire the other language.[8]

Role of Age: some researchers, including Noam Chomsky opine that age plays a role to learn L2. Though L1 happens through acquisition, L2 is age specific. Once the learners are past a critical period i.e. puberty, they lose the capacity to acquire subconsciously L2. The process is not implicit like the L1. The second language is to be gained explicitly. For, the ability to implicitly gain the L2 declines gradually due to the fear of doing wrong. They (learners) do not experiment in L2 by venturing as it is a risky job. Risky in the sense, they will have to face the risk of awkwardness, if something goes wrong in their speech or articulation in public.

In the case of the socially elite in India, they acquire English as if it is their mother tongue. For, their social conditions promote contact with English language speakers and it affords them opportunities to learn or acquire better. In the case of rural downtrodden children, they do not get such opportunities in their vicinity.

1. N. Krishnaswamy 1971, An Introduction to Linguistics for Language Teachers, Somaiya Publications Pvt Ltd, 172, Naigaum Cross Road, Dardar, Bombay-14DD. pp.212-13

2. Teaching as 'input', Exploring Language Pedagogy through Second Language Acquisition Research, Rod Ellis and Natsuko Shintani, Routledge Introductions to Applied Linguistics, *Exploring Language Pedagogy through Second Language Acquisition Research - (2014).pdf) pp.189-190 /401

3. COMO FAZER UMA CITAÇÃO DESTA PÁGINA: Schütz, Ricardo E. "Stephen Krashen's Theory of Second Language Acquisition" English Made in Brazil <https://www.sk.com.br/sk-krash-english.html>. Online. *(data do acesso).*

4. Teaching as 'input', Exploring Language Pedagogy through Second Language Acquisition Research, Rod Ellis and Natsuko Shintani, Routledge Introductions to Applied Linguistics, *Exploring Language Pedagogy through Second Language Acquisition Research - (2014).pdf) pp.[1] 190/401

5. National Curriculum Framework 2005, National Council for Educational Research and Training (NCERT), New Delhi. p.40

6. N. Krishnaswamy 1971, An Introduction to Linguistics for Language Teachers p-212-13, Somaiya Publications Pvt Ltd, 172, Naigaum Cross Road, Dadar, Bombay-14DD. P.122

7. Ibid. p. 122

8. https://youtu.be/AkXK2CqB3No

iii. Eminent Linguists' views on the use of L1 in L2 (English class)

There are many English teachers in India that use the learners L1 to teach the learners' L2 i.e. English. From English to English, teaching is rare and is also not totally desirable in the Indian context. However, there are theories by experts in linguistics, how much of L1 could be used in the English classroom. If English teachers are asked whether to use mother tongue/L1 in English class, they come out with different views. Because English teachers have been guided to teach English in a monolingual method i.e. using English-only in the class. The British Council did a survey of English teachers on using L1 in the class.

"...the British Council's 'Teaching English' web page (2009). The web page asked whether the respondents agreed with these two statements:

1. If we use L1 in language teaching, learners will become dependent on L1, and not even try to understand meaning from context and explanation,

or

2. say what they want to say within their limited command of the target language (L2).

The two statements encapsulate two of the reasons frequently given for and against the use of the L1.

On the one hand, using the L1 deprives learners of the opportunity to experience communicating in the L2 but, on the other hand, it helps to alleviate the anxiety that arises when communicating with limited linguistic resources."[1]

In any case, as an English teacher, I view, if the affective filters are low, L2 learners would learn the target language effectively and the L1 can be used by the teacher on an ad hoc basis wherever it is necessary.

L1 in the English class - views of eminent linguists:

Cook (2001, p. 413) argues for judicious use of the L1 in the teaching of second or foreign languages but cautions that despite the legitimacy of using the L1 under certain conditions, "it is clearly useful to employ large quantities of the L2..."[2]

Turnbull (2001) responded to Cook by acknowledging that while there is a place for teachers to use students' L1 in second and foreign language teaching, there are major disadvantages when teachers rely too extensively on the L1. Specifically, when teachers who may not be highly fluent in L2 are given the "green light" to use students' L1, then L2 use in the classroom may decline significantly on the part of both teachers and students.[3]

Prabhu (1987) identified three types of tasks (to use L1) … information-gap, an opinion-gap, or a reasoning-gap.[4] These tasks regularly teachers make learners do.

Macaro (2011) claimed that the issue of whether teachers should codeswitch is 'the most important theoretical and pedagogic question facing both the research and practitioner communities today".[5]

There was discussion to use L1 as a mediational tool in English language teaching. Code-switching is one of the prominent methods of using L1 in the English class. In code-switching, the teacher uses mother tongue/L1 to make the learner understand what she is saying in English lowering the bar of affective-filter. Given an option, most students prefer their mother tongue/L1 to teach English. There are a number of different terms that can be used to refer to the use of the learners' mother tongue in the L2 classroom i.e. 'L1 use', 'codeswitching', 'own-language use'.[6]

To sum up the use of L1 in the L2 English class is still a matter of discussion. How much to be used and what amount, is even now an unsettled matter for the linguists, researchers and teachers. As an English teacher, I experienced many of my students of the mother tongue/regional medium asking me to explain what was in the lesson in their L1. They also assured me that they could fare well in the English examination, once they know everything in the lesson in their mother tongue. My answer was always in the negative. If I had agreed to what they had asked for, my English classes would have become once again L1 classes for them. My learners' request was perhaps to avoid the amount of stress they had to take in understanding each and everything in English.

---

1. Exploring Language Pedagogy through Second Language Acquisition Research Rod Ellis and Natsuko Shintani, Routledge Introductions to Applied Linguistics, *Exploring Language Pedagogy through Second Language Acquisition Research - (2014).pdf) p.239

2. "Rethinking monolingual instructional strategies in multilingual classrooms", Jim Cummins, Ontario Institute for Studies in Education, p. 223, University of Toronto*7-vol-10-no2-art-cummins monolingual ill-effects.pdf pp.3/20

3. Ibid p. 223,

4. Exploring Language Pedagogy through Second Language Acquisition Research, Rod Ellis and Natsuko Shintani, Routledge Introductions to Applied Linguistics, *Exploring Language Pedagogy through Second Language Acquisition Research - (2014).pdf) p.160

5. Ibid p.239

6. Ibid p.260

Chapter-4

As English Second Language Teacher-Difficulties Faced

Many in India agree that the knowledge in English is beneficial. Therefore, to learn the English language students would leave no stone unturned. For them, the easiest way to get marks is to mug some standard answers from prescribed reading passages or lessons given in text to produce the same in the examination. To write on their own is very difficult. The English language vocabulary and structure are extensive. However, the grammar tells how to arrange words in particular order in English. Again, vocabulary has a gradation according to the class they are in. When it comes to expression, the graded vocabulary and grammar that they acquire during the course is not sufficient. Coming to spelling, there is no other way than to transcribe it or to commit to their memory. That being the case, the academicians in India have set marks/grades that a student should get in English are on par with that of the mother tongue. This is setting a high benchmark.

The usual errors committed by students of ESL, while writing and understanding grammar, is note-worthy. In the case of English-medium students, the silent acquisition from varied sources: like that of the science, social studies, mathematics subjects that are being taught in English enhances their capability. This is learning language across the curriculum. Their formation of sentences or expression of ideas are much easier. To them there are opportunities to explore their potential in the language. Many students that study English as a second or third language raise doubts, often on the language, that is unusual and unheard of. Let's take grammar first.

Articles: a, an, the, are taught carefully, from the beginning from lower classes onwards. This is for habit formation to use articles, when they grow up speaking or writing English. Yet, the articles are the most omitted ones, in speech or writing by many Indians. The main reason being, they are not found in Indian languages. People, often grown-ups, keep questioning by saying, you call an apple as - 'apple' (dropping the article) in mother tongue, why should we say 'an' apple in English? It is quite odd in the Indian context, they argue. They are often told: an apple is any apple. 'The apple' - is a particular apple. Hence, articles make meaning. As a consequence, the indefinite and definite articles make sense in English. They are specific to the language. Yet, dropping of articles is a common phenomenon in India. Whereas, most European languages carry articles.

This specificity of articles, though students grasp, they do not pay attention to while speaking or writing, as they are not present in their mother tongue. Nonetheless, English teachers do need to teach them. Occasionally, dropping the article by anyone, would not matter, and it in no way changes the meaning of what they are saying. A teacher ritualistically teaches how to place articles i.e. explaining what to use before vowel or consonant sounds. Any amount of explanation regarding 'article-usage', is of no avail. Interestingly, the same was expressed by Michael Swan in his 'Basic English Usage'. He writes, 'The correct use of the articles (a/an/the) is one of the most difficult points in English grammar. Fortunately, most article mistakes do not matter too much. Even if we leave all the articles out of a sentence, it is usually possible to understand it.' He then adds, 'However, it is better to use the articles correctly if possible.'[1]

For instance:

1. I went to railway station to buy ticket to Chennai (incorrect)

2. I went to the railway station to buy a ticket to Chennai (correct)

Both sentences make sense. But the English language demands specific (a ticket) and definite (the railway station) articles to give clarity.

Hence, teaching of articles is necessary for English language teachers but omission of articles, at times, by students is not a punishable error. Many western European languages i.e. French, German, Dutch, Spanish etc., have articles in their languages like in English. For this reason, article-features are not a problem for them, while learning English. On the other hand, Indians do have a problem.

To begin with, the teacher teaches indefinite and definite articles and the rules where they have to be placed. Again, mandatorily she teaches the vowels and consonants in English. Indefinite article: 'a' before a word that starts with a consonant. And 'an' before a word that starts with a vowel. Giving examples like: The Sun, the moon, the stars etc., to show how to place definite articles to definite things in the universe. Of course, there are several exceptions to these rules of placing articles. Cumbersome procedure. Yet, in the Indian context, it is good to teach the rules.

Use of Universal Grammar (UG)

Universal Grammar (UG) can be effectively used in English Grammar class. For, the fundamental elements: parts of speech are the same for any language. A teacher could use L1 equivalents to make students understand. In any case, the concrete nouns could be easily understood. When it comes to the categorisation of nouns in English, things complicate. Different kinds of nouns: the proper nouns to be written beginning with capital letters and the common nouns to begin with a small letter, shows the specificity of English language. Apart from those, the collective nouns of various hues are all meant for conscious learning. Collective nouns should be committed to memory. Abstract nouns are almost vague. These demarcations of nouns are not consciously learnt in their mother tongue/ L 1. Moreover, Indian languages have no capitalisation. Indian languages have no stress on syllables. Hence, accent is one definitive feature for the English language. That becomes difficult for Indians. Whatever effort learners make in the classroom with regard to pronunciation and accent, that's not sufficient. As a result, testing the accent and pronunciation of words in the examination again, is a gamble. Usually, L 2 English learners, often learn exercises that are given for pronunciation in their English Reader. Because, the same is repeated in their examination paper. Even if, occasionally, an audio or video of pronunciation is shown that may not last long in their memory. Now, in this age of internet connection and free mobile data availability, the scenario has changed. The interested students could have a Dictionary app that gives correct pronunciation.

Is and was

The difficulties I faced in teaching English were all of my experiential domain. Some are: primarily with verbs, i.e., maintaining appropriate tense for the situation. Though, from class-1 onwards, students get sentences with is or was, as the main verb, they still have confusion. When asked to narrate an incident, they cannot use proper verbs. One of my students, out of her utter confusion, whether to use 'is or was' in a sentence, she has written both. She used both in her written-answer- script with a stroke (oblique) in between i.e. is/was, for me to select the one I needed. I understood her dilemma. Learning in artificially contrived situations, with no use of English language outside, these problems crop up. Especially in the case of mother-tongue medium students. What she did was not correct. She could have selected one (is or was) right or wrong. This mistake was not in one place. Throughout the answer sheet she continued with that perplexity using the two. That student was an intelligent student and scored well in all subjects. When I asked her why she did what she did, she was perturbed. She posed a naïve question to me. She asked me, 'What is the meaning of "is and was" in Telugu?' I was a little perplexed. Because, they are not content words to carry some meaning. Since they are structure words, I said they represent the present or past condition in which the action is taking place, explaining some situations. That did not go down well with her, as the tense has many forms. Is and was are used to state the condition as well as auxiliary verbs in the present/ past progressive forms. Such auxiliary forms are not found in Telugu. Students, especially the ESL ones, think that every word should have a meaning. Unless they understand the meaning, they cannot understand the language. Though the English pedagogy shifted to descriptive grammar and communicative approach, even in this approach students come out with doubts that are unheard of.

Sometimes, is and was are used together. Some seasoned English columnists use is/was together in a sentence in their writings. That indicates that something was present then and is also now, instead of using 'has been' for continuing. This they do deliberately, separating the past and present and indicating them in equal measure. For instance: Corruption was and is a malice practiced in the country. This may indicate, in one sense, that corruption was there in the previous regime and is still continuing now. Strangely, many educated Indians also use: is and was, indiscriminately. To introduce their friend that studied years ago in school with them, they say: 'He is my classmate in school', instead of: 'He was my classmate in school'. Perhaps, to them, to use or to associate past (was) with a person at present living is tabooed. If he was a dead person, they may be using: 'He was my classmate'. English is tricky in this way to use the past for a dead person or a past association with a present person alive. I cannot vouch for all Indian languages, but in Telugu, for the past and the present: He is my classmate, does work. Telugu people come to know about, when he was or when he is the classmate, with reference to now or then used, in the sentence. So, children getting confused about the appropriate tense has many dimensions.

Reported Speech

The reported speech is otherwise called indirect speech. For many students, this is a problematic area. Reported speech in writing has to undergo several changes and challenges. While speaking, the same reporting i.e. what somebody said, is easy to say. The critical changes of tense in writing are not needed in speaking. While speaking in English, there is a mix of all tenses. You narrate an incident based on what you had said and others had answered in their own words. Sometimes say others' words directly or indirectly by changing it into a report. For this, there are no inverted commas, no complicated tense changes, as is in the case of written English. A student's performance is always assessed in the written-examination only. Hence, students of ESL take pains in learning how to report.

Suppose a student is given a sentence, for instance: Mr Ashok said, "The country has been witnessing horrible deaths due to Covid-19." In the examination, if the student is asked to report the same, she needs to completely change it to: Mr Ashok said that the country had been witnessing horrible deaths due to Covid-19. Look, if the Covid-19 pandemic is still continuing while Mr Ashok was speaking and even after that the scene has not changed, why should the verb be changed? - is the dilemma. But, while reporting what the person said, was to be taken into that particular context. And whatever he said has to be changed into past tense because the entire thing is in the past. What the other person is doing, is reporting what he said without bothering, whether the said conditions are prevailing even now and accordingly to keep the tense or to change the tense. This is as per the English language. In Indian languages, these awkward changes are not necessary.

Coming to the students' examinations, if out of five changes that are to be made from a direct-sentence to an indirect or reported speech, if one or two are unable to be made by a student in the examination, the whole thing is struck down as wrong and she/he gets a zero-mark. This amount of accuracy cannot be expected from the ESL student. The reported speech is mainly meant for a student to learn how to report someone's speech. In the due process, the changes they make: from first person to third person, tense form according to the reporting verb etc., do help them in real life while speaking English. When they are given the question at a sentence level to be reported, each change a student makes should be awarded some points, instead of demanding the whole sentence to report correctly. These reporting should be at paragraph level rather than at sentence level. That makes for a better understanding.

There is so much tentativeness in language. If a sentence is like:

My uncle said, "I will come to your house today."

If the same sentence has to be reported the same day:

My uncle said that he would come to my house that day ---would be odd. 'Will' and 'today' need not be changed, if it is on the same day. Yet, it is done as per conventional grammar.

Relative clauses:

A curious question on relative clauses:

While I was teaching relative clauses, a student asked me a thought-provoking question. Her doubt was, as to why a wh-word (like who/ which/where etc.,) that has to be at the beginning of a question, is in the middle of the sentence? The relative pronouns are question-words for her. I could perceive her genuine quest. The relative pronouns (who, whom, which, where, when, whose) are introduced as question- words or interrogative pronouns in questions. But their function in the relative clauses is that of a relative pronoun. Though academic experts say not to use grammatical labels, the doubt raised about wh-word coming in the middle of the sentence, makes a teacher doubtful of how to go about.

This is how I would explain my students:

Relative pronouns appear regularly in the next part of the sentence, that is in the second part i.e., in the relative clause. So, they refer to the name of a person, animal, place or a thing that is in the first part of the sentence. Since they relate to a noun in the first part, they are doing the job of a pronoun. A pronoun is used instead of a noun.

For instance: I saw the grammar book, which was on the table in the morning.

Here which is used instead of the book (a noun) again. So, therefore, in the place of a noun: the book, 'which', is used as a pronoun. And that pronoun is showing the relationship with the noun mentioned in the earlier part of the sentence (the book), hence 'which' is a relative pronoun. The second part: 'which was on the table in the morning', is not a complete sentence because it is not giving complete meaning. It cannot stand on its own. So, it depends on the first part. The first part: 'I saw the grammar book', is a sentence by itself and is independent. The second part depends on it. So, therefore it is a clause not a sentence. As it starts with a relative pronoun, it is a relative clause. Like all clauses it depends on the main clause. All this explanation is needed.

Wh-words are used both as: interrogative pronouns (while framing questions) and as relative pronouns (in the relative clauses). A student can understand that a pronoun is a word used in the place of a noun. Students can also understand: he, she, and it being pronouns and how they replace nouns. But can they know: that, who, which, where, when, whom etc. ---why are they called pronouns? They need explanation, as they are consciously learning English grammar.

Again, the question-words: who, whom, which, where, when, whose, etc., are pronouns in the category of 'interrogative pronouns. They are at the beginning of the sentence. Students know functionally that they are all question-words. Why are they called pronouns needs a different explanation. *who* represents a person, *which* represents a thing, *where* represents a place, *when* represents time and *whose* represents the person's possession. On that account, they are all representing and replacing the nouns. Thus, they are pronouns.

For instance: if someone says:

I want that book (pointing to a particular book, when there are many).

Immediately the other person trying to help out but not knowing which book, asks: which one?

'Which' replaces 'that particular book', so it is a pronoun.

Similarly, for the question:

Q) Who built the Taj mahal?

Ans) Shah Jahan built the Taj Mahal.

Here, 'who' is used to know the person who built the Taj Mahal i.e., Shah Jahan. 'Who' has replaced Shah Jahan. For that reason, it is a pronoun but interrogative in nature. Surprisingly, these details need not be explained. Won't it cause more confusion than clarity? Without knowing all these aspects many speak good English. Therefore, labelling grammatical items is not needed is the opinion of many academicians.

Though grammar is taught descriptively, in a context or situation, contrived or real, these occasional labelling occurs. For inquisitive learners of English as a second or third language, these doubts are inevitable. Especially those that study in a regional medium, try to understand each grammatical item taught in detail. Otherwise, they think they are incapable of learning a foreign language. Earlier, in olden days parsing of a sentence was in vogue. That had not done much good to the acquisition of English language or to use it in their real-life situations.

Defining and Non-Defining Relative Clauses/Adjectival Clauses:

After all the explanation on relative pronouns, another tougher part is, the defining and non-defining relative clauses. For example:

1. The old man who worked in our neighbour's house as a gardener was actually a rich man.

2. Raju, who worked in my house as a driver for many years, died last night.

Both sentences above have relative pronouns and have relative clauses. Both clauses are embedded in the sentences. In the first one: who worked in the neighbour's house, is defining the old man. So, it is a Defining Relative Clause. In the second one: who worked in my house as a driver for many years, is adding extra information about Raju without which the sentence: Raju died last night, is sufficient. Hence, it is a Non-Defining Relative Clause. In both cases, these relative clauses are talking about the persons (nouns), mentioned earlier. So, something that talks about the noun is an adjective. Therefore, these clauses are also called adjectival clauses. The difference is subtle. In both sentences the relative clauses seem to be defining the persons (The old man and Raju) and both seem to be providing extra information. The technicality provided to them to describe the second sentence is: commas.

This much nitty-gritty is needed to teach one-grammatical item to the students of class-IX, in a regional medium class of English. The input given by the teacher with all explanations may not be the in-take of many students. This is all to obtain one-mark in the examination, when tested on relative clauses. Sometimes the relative-clause question may not appear in the question paper at all. Nevertheless, the knowledge relating to it is helpful to the student in her life. But how many teachers who teach ESL students are thorough with English grammar, when they study English as second language? If they have not had an understandable input in school, it becomes too difficult to teach.

In all teacher-orientation classes, teachers are advised not to teach formal grammatical labels in the class. They say that will intimidate the students. Just a descriptive explanation is sufficient for them. Yet, without knowing and labelling the parts of speech in English nothing could be taught. They should know how they function. Without which their wh-question in the case of relative clauses cannot be answered. There are grammar exercises in all textbooks. Therefore, conscious grammar learning has become a part of the curriculum.

Active and Passive Voice

Voice is another important aspect of English grammar. In India, schools and office circulars most often start with passive sentences, like: It is noticed... or it is observed...or it has been brought to the notice of...etc. Traditionally, voice has been taught to students from ages in India. Active and passive voice can be easily explained as mathematical equations: when the active voice sentence is passivized the following changes take place. The subject becomes the object and the object becomes the subject, the verb changes. How to change simple present, progressive, perfect etc. by adding forms. But however, it is not as simple as this explanation. The students have to do vast exercises for getting one mark in the examination on active and passive voice related question, despite the pressure of other subjects: like mathematics, science and social studies. In spite of their hours of work on voice, they sometimes get the following kind of questions on voice:

For e.g., Has a dog ever bitten you?

It is an interrogative sentence not a statement.

To passivize an interrogative sentence is more difficult than a statement. A student of ESL background finds it very difficult. The first step is to passivize and to make it into a statement like:

You have ever been bitten by a dog?

Next, since it's a question, the student needs to put it in the question form, by fronting the 'have'. Now, the correct form is:

Have you ever been bitten by a dog?

Learning tediously these language items of English is undue for a school student. Schools are not exclusive English institutions. Many times, being a teacher, I asked the standard question paper-setter of English Board Examinations, why they had allotted only one mark to this question? That one mark also, a student gets, if all the complicated changes are fully made. That is the rule. If the student perfectly changes with no grammatical errors, then only, the allotted mark will be awarded. In that case, why is half a mark not given, if a student makes half of the changes? That means: subject to object and object to subject, even if she goes wrong in changing the verb. For each one or half a mark counts in the Board examinations. The student's future depends on it. After all, English could be learnt later in life, if they could get through their Board examinations that certify their school-leaving. Suppose, if they fail, they need to write the supplementary examinations. That would be difficult as they leave the school and nobody to guide them. And they needed to prepare on their own without the teacher's help. Students get demoralized when they fail by one or two marks. These students come to School-final Board examinations, with no detention-system in earlier classes in all state government-run schools. As a consequence, the teachers teaching for the Board examination would face an uphill task to teach them. For, they are not well-equipped with English-skills that they needed to acquire in their previous classes/standards. Though there is a gradation in syllabus, as far as grammar and vocabulary are concerned, many learners would not reach up to the mark. Free-promotion policy to the higher class every year with no detention, would not result in expected outcomes, especially in English.

Phrasal Verbs

Coming to phrasal verbs i.e. verb and particle together give an entirely different meaning. Though introduced in a graded manner, they have an inherent difficulty. Again, they are specific to the English language. There is an anecdotal reference on how phrasal verb goof-ups cause serious meaning change. To give clarity, there is an anecdote … once a professor was sitting in his chamber. He saw his colleague passing by his room. An unknown person came later and enquired about his colleague's whereabouts. The professor immediately said, "He just passed away", waving his hand in that direction. Passed by and passed away have two entirely different meanings. With the word: pass, we get many phrasal verbs. How could a student of ESL learn and keep them all in memory?

It is said that someone asked the renowned English writer R.K. Narayan, what is the most difficult item in the English language? He said: prepositions. The correct prepositions, an Englishman uses, may not be acquired by a non-native speaker. Nevertheless, students in school are tested with some of the general, most recurrent prepositions, which they often encounter in their speech or writing. But there is an inherent difficulty in learning phrasal verbs.

For e.g.

i.   burst **out** laughing and burst **into** tears,

ii. died **of** cancer and died **at** the age of nineteen…

These kinds of subtle differences cannot be learnt in bits and pieces. Even if the teacher contextualizes in the class, that may not last long in memory. The student needs to make extra effort in English-reading and acquiring.

If-Conditionals Clauses

If-conditionals pose problems to students. In the three-types of if-conditional clauses, the first one seems to be the easiest for students. The second conditional is specific to the English language alone. For, it is not found in most of the Indian languages.

Conditional-II

For e.g.

i.   If I became a doctor, I would treat the poor patients freely.

ii. If I were you, I wouldn't do that work.

The sentences of the above kind are unknown constructions to ESL students. The subjunctive ' 'were" is new to them, as 'I' - is followed by am in the present or was in the past tense but not with a were. These changes should be taught explicitly.

The grown-ups often use it in their conversation: I was thinking…and continue in the present tense the rest of the sentence.

For instance:

i.   I was wondering what is happening in this studio debate...

ii. I was wondering when you will start the program

iii. I was wondering why you are asking such an absurd question

iv. I was wondering if you all can plan a picnic.

Although, the above sentences at the start give reference to the past, they are used frequently to refer to a present thought. Unless students thoroughly immerse themselves in the language, it is difficult for them to speak or write these kinds of sentences. When someone does not know the language, their communication hampers. Of course, the third-conditional is not so much of a problem for students to understand.

Grammar is the skeleton of the language and the flesh and blood are provided by the content. In any competitive examination, including in the Teacher Eligibility Test (TET), grilling and gruelling questions on English grammar are given. Once when I enquired some of the teachers preparing to write the teacher eligibility test, on how they were preparing for the English examination paper, their answer was amusing! They said they were preparing content subjects like science, mathematics, social studies, psychology and pedagogy more, and for English they were not paying attention, as they thought it would be a waste of time. They said, they would not waste time on English grammar. In any case, the examination would be in objective type and they could tick their choice of answer, then and there, by guesswork. They said they could select from among the multiple choices given, as they deem fit. If luck favours that would be the correct choice. Instead of sitting hours together with English grammar and its minute details, they thought they could concentrate on other subjects in which they were sure of getting marks. Most of the candidates I enquired, that were appearing for the teacher eligibility test, were all from regional medium background. And they all accepted the difficulty of learning English grammar.

---

1. Michael Swan, 'Basic English Usage', OXFORD University Press 2011, YMCA Building, Jai Singh Road, New Delhi 11001 pp.37-38

Chapter-5

English Only as a Subject in School-Difficulties of Students

For most schoolchildren in India who pursue studies in their mother tongue or regional language, English as a subject is difficult, after mathematics. Of course, mathematics is a knowledge subject and English is a skill-based one. For understanding and solving problems in mathematics intellect is needed. On the other hand, for acquiring the skills of English, aptitude and exposure to the language, are the prime requisites. The various doubts expressed by students in the English class, while learning the language, makes an English teacher wonder. This happens in higher classes with inquisitive students. It goes without saying, for English teachers in India, English is not their mother tongue. For almost all, their mother tongue is one of the Indian languages. Moreover, their own English by way of pronunciation, articulation, spelling and grammar are somewhat questionable, barring a small section that acquired the right kind, by studying in convents of repute. For most of the English teachers, it is an acquired language not a natural one. Here, I do not mean language should be taught by native speakers. Only the Indian English teachers know the specific problem faced by Indian students.

To learn the English language, students put in hard work. For them the easiest way to get marks is to mug some standard answers to reading passages or lessons given in text and the same to reproduce in the examination. To write on their own a few sentences is a big task. The English language and vocabulary are very vast. However, English grammar tells how to arrange words in a particular order and rules that are in place and also many exceptions to those rules. When it comes to expression, the graded vocabulary and grammar that they acquire during the course is not sufficient to communicate. Communication in a language is like driving on the road. Usually, teachers are so secure of their students, they always try to prepare the road for them to drive. Instead what they should do is to prepare them for the road. That is, a student needs to negotiate or navigate the road outside on her own while driving i.e. in communicating. The road and the traffic are never constant. They keep changing. Similarly, communication outside the classroom depends on situations they encounter. Here, structuring and communicating play a role. When it comes to spelling, there is no other way other than to transcribe it or commit it to (their) memory by rote.

That being the case, the academicians in India have set marks/grades that a student should obtain in English subject, to be on par with that of their mother tongue or regional language. This is something to be examined. Most of the mother tongue or regional medium students, learn certain questions and answers. They learn poems in English by rote. And also learn certain grammatical rules. By doing so, an average student scores marks to pass in the examination. In spite of that, higher authorities in academic circles/policy-makers say, 'uniform tests that assess *memorized facts* and *textbook based learning* are obsolete'. Meaning to say it is outdated and it should not be encouraged. What is the way out? For any average student in a school, writing an answer on her own in English is difficult. Moreover, if the student is from a mother tongue or regional medium, her minimum language exposure would not allow. She cannot deliberately think in English. Often mother tongue intrudes into the flow of thought.

Sometimes, open-ended questions are asked in the examination. The formation of sentences following grammar and conveying meaning in itself is a huge task. This they need to do then and there in the examination. Just think over … for drafting, a small letter or an excerpt on any event in English, adults take so much time. They make so many edits before making it final. Accordingly, for a student from a mother tongue/regional medium background to expect answers freely to write, is setting the bar high. There is no denying that some smart students come out with ideas and write in English but that is not the case in general. As a goal or ideal, to tap creativity in the second language is good. Towards that end teachers should strive. However, free-writing in English should be done at leisure. During the examination, at least a fifty-percent-mark allotment needs to be for the memorized items. Once the students get through the examinations, they will have ample time in life to learn English. As a teacher, I feel, to demote students is to deprive them of further education, just because they could not express themselves in English. This is no good in the larger cause of education.

Many experts suggest, instead of actual time-fixed examinations that encourage rote-learning, 'a continuous comprehensive evaluation (CCE)' and 'careful observation' are the remedies to be followed. For this, the teacher's role is made more responsible. She needs to be a careful observer and has to assess from time to time how a student is performing. This observation needs dedication. Only those teachers well-versed in the English language and devoted to their profession could do so. Otherwise, the standard tools i.e., tests/examinations which are written in nature are more accurate to evaluate. The Continuous Comprehensive Evaluation (CCE) is in the hands of the teacher in the classroom. It becomes a subjective tool. For most teachers, teaching is a job, not a profession. Teachers are no different from any other government-employees, in any government department. Diligent teachers do a continuous process of assessment of their students in schools. Yet, the laxity of some others, becomes a contagion in a system, where there is no reward for hard-work and no punishment for the otherwise engaged. Of course, teaching well is self-rewarding, as the teacher finds fulfilment in her work. If a student understands what the teacher teaches, it will be evident from her face, if the teacher properly observes. It gives immense satisfaction to the teacher. It's also self-congratulatory for a teacher, when all students get through the examinations that are externally evaluated. These are the feel-good factors, for each and every individual teacher, that teaches with dedication and devotion to her profession.

Let us observe some other difficulties of ESL

The frozen English:

Students of ESL learn formulaic expressions or social formulas.

For instance, if they are asked: how are you?

They say: I am fine, thank you.

And in return sometimes: how are you?

Some teachers correct them by saying, only for: how do you do- type, you need to reciprocate, by saying: how do you do? Not for how are you? - type ones.

Most of the debates among teachers are on formula-like sentences rather than on the larger picture of communication. Of course, it is necessary to learn greetings and other mannerisms/etiquette according to English style because it is specific to that language.

How do you do? – type of greetings, whether they are formulaic or not, de Saussure called them *ready-made utterances.* For, these expressions which are learned as unanalysable wholes and employed on particular occasions by native speakers. How do you do?, which, though it is conventionally punctuated as a question, is not normally interpreted as such; and unlike genuine questions beginning *How do you* ..., constructed by means of the productive rules of English grammar...Another 'ready-made' English expression is *Rest in peace* (as a tombstone inscription) which, unlike for example *Rest here quietly for a moment,* is not regarded as an instruction or suggestion made to the person, one is addressing, but a situationally-bound expression which is unanalysable grammatical structure of contemporary English.'[1]

In the same way, *God bless you!* God is not grammatically the third person singular here that takes the inflectional –es (blesses).[2] Perhaps this 'God bless you' comes from the expression: 'May God bless you' in which case, 'may' might have been dropped in usage. These ready-made utterances are prefabricated ones specific to languages of all linguistic communities.

'The stock of proverbs passed on from one generation to the next provides many instances of 'ready-made utterances'.[3] For e.g. First come, first serve, Easy come easy go, a stitch in time saves nine etc. their internal structure, unlike genuine sentences, is not as per rules which specify the right combination of words. This expression permits no extension or variation. There are also other grammatically unstructured or partly structured utterances that we use. For instance:

What is the use of...? Or for ... sake. They are the schemata. When they are in combination in a sentence, they go by rules of grammar'.[4]

For e.g.

1. What's the use of going to school late?

2. What's the use of a carrying mask, if it is not worn?

3. What's the use of online classes, if we can't meet each other?

4. I am doing this work for my mother's sake.

5. For my family's sake I need to earn more money.

Widdowson, after a lengthy discussion of formulaic language, claims that learners need to know how to apply "a scale of variability" to grammar rules. Communicative competence is a matter of knowing a stock of partially pre-assembled patterns, formulaic frameworks, and a kit of rules, so to speak, and being able to apply the rules to make whatever adjustments are necessary according to contextual demands (Widdowson, 1989).[5]

Formulaic frameworks are language-specific. They include:

1. Idioms: e.g. 'to make both ends meet' --- to have adequate money,

2. Collocations e.g.: bread and butter, table and chair etc.,

3. Proverbs –e.g.: make hay while the sun shines.

4. Some catchy –phrases e.g., last but not least i.e. not less important.

5. Quotations of great men: these we use as they are, without changing any word, hence formula-like.

These are all with regard to sentences. At word-level, learning new vocabulary along with spelling is one of the difficult aspects of English language learning. Now, let us see one by one what the problems of ESL students are. The first biggest hurdle is spelling. As there is no one to one correspondence between pronunciation and writing in English, spelling has to be learnt consciously by rote or by transcription. In this data-driven- internet- social media-age, the lingo of the youngsters has changed. They are used to short-messaging. Nevertheless, the teachers insist that they use spelling and grammar systematically. Before the fad of sending social media-short messages, they need to know the English language thoroughly. Then they could mend, twist or turn language items to suit their whim (in the social media or elsewhere) in their chosen minimalist way. Even in English -speaking countries, mistakes are galore in the writings of children and adults. The former US President Donald Trump was famous for spelling goof-ups on his Twitter-messages! His confused spelling during the 2020 election, for: polls, as poles, made even the non-English-speaking world wonder![6] Subsequently, he was trolled on Twitter the very next moment.

Regarding the English language learning in India, grammar plays a vital role. The ESL students are taught overtly grammatical rules most often. Even while teaching in a communicative method (of teaching English), the students need an overt explanation of grammar rules. Whereas, English medium students are taught covertly through a situational- communicative method. They already have a tacit understanding of grammar rules as they are exposed to language learning through other subjects of the curriculum viz. science, mathematics, social sciences etc., still, in the words of the famous linguists Gumperz and John J, grammar is needed. They argue that 'the concept of language-usage, is for conveying important social information and is therefore not a matter of individual choice (i.e. the way randomly speaking) but must be rule-governed.'[7] In their research paper they differentiate: linguistic competence (ability to produce grammatically correct sentences) from communicative competence (ability to select appropriate forms from the totality of grammatically correct expressions available). That means, even if schoolchildren of the mother tongue/local medium learn rules of grammar, they must be able to select appropriate forms to communicate. That is, they need to use it more and more in their daily lives.

According to Stephen Krashen, this rule-governed or rule-emphasized method of teaching would not yield communication. For him communication has to take place naturally. Imagine, in India, we learn other Indian languages easily without knowing grammar rules. If our neighbour is a Marathi or Gujarati or a Tamil-speaking, and if I am not from any of that language group, I could easily learn their language by listening to them speaking in their language. First, I may pick up some words, then sentence structure etc., because I know the basic rules of sentence formation in my mother tongue. That is not happening in the case of English in India. Krashen, when he says, 'Language acquisition does not require extensive use of conscious grammatical rules, and does not require tedious drill,'[8] he might have meant this. He further adds, 'Acquisition requires meaningful interaction in the target language ... natural communication ... in which speakers are concerned not with the form of their utterances but with the messages they are conveying and understanding.'[9] Of course, in India, English teachers are advised so, in all in-service training programmes. Here, 'interaction in target language' and 'natural communication' are crucial. Both are not possible to a great extent in the Indian context.

In the ESL class, interaction is mostly done in the local language. Whatever the teacher speaks in English by way of communication, is not natural by any means. Teachers contrive (artificial) situations, solely for the purpose of speaking in English. Given an opportunity, the teacher naturally shifts to her mother tongue or regional language, in order to make herself understood to students. For teaching a lesson in English, the teacher does homework to that extent, in English usually. That is, she prepares for class with her limited repertoire of English knowledge. Next, Krashen's theories of language learning are possible in a relaxed situation and also when the learner is self-motivated to learn a language. In school education in India, English is a compulsory subject. Failure in English meant failure in other subjects too, as the student would not obtain a pass-certificate. Hence, there is an external pressure to learn and perform in the examination. A teacher cannot teach or patiently wait for some language acquisition to take place. So, therefore, rightly or wrongly, English becomes a subject like any other subject to be taught, so as to make a student get a good grade in the school-final examination. At the beginning, the hurdle is the examination. Once a student gets through that, much could be earned later in life.

As far as Krashen's statement ... 'comprehensible input' is the crucial and necessary ingredient for the acquisition of language,'[10] is correct. This comprehensible input is pre-decided and made available to the student in the form of: textbook, supplementary reader etc. A teacher needs to complete an a priori (prepared earlier) syllabus. Many teachers depend on textbooks faithfully not because it was a top-down order, but because they follow the convention. In any case, very few are capable of making their own materials to teach. To make text-material on their own, teachers need to know the underlying principles of language. Such extensive details many are not aware of. On the other hand, often in all in-service programmes, teachers are advised to go by methods (not the material) of their own that make the schoolchildren reach the aims of teaching English language. Quite often, teachers are encouraged to make teaching material nowadays, but this is in addition to the textbook material provided to them.

Let's see this analogy. In the computer, the menu-bar is at the top of the MS Word-file. In it, we find pull-down menus for e.g.: File, Edit, Review, View, Insert etc. They are all coded and arranged by the programmer. The user takes the item required for his use from among them, whatever is suitable for her purpose. In the same way, textbooks are prepared by experts in the field and teachers use them for their benefit in the classroom interaction.

Krashen's theory, 'The best methods are therefore those that supply 'comprehensible input' in low anxiety situations, containing messages that students really want to hear. These methods do not force early production in the second language, but allow students to produce when they are 'ready', recognizing that improvement comes from supplying communicative and comprehensible input, and not from forcing and correcting production.'[11] However, in an ideal situation, when someone is intrinsically motivated to learn a language, at his own pace, this logic of learning by Krashen suits. When an English teacher is allotted only forty or forty-five minutes of time each day to teach in school, her mission almost always will be in completing the periodic annual syllabus within the time-period given. Anyhow, in it all skills are graded, for all schoolchildren of the age/grade to learn.

For any language learning, you need to have a conducive student-friendly atmosphere. Since most of the English teachers know this (and are also often advised in their in-service-programmes), they keep the class accordingly. Hence, they take up play-way methods in primary classes, group-activities, pair-drills, peer-reviews in higher forms. Teachers are often reminded that their role is that of a facilitator in the teaching-learning process. Since most of the English teachers come from the same background as that of the students, they know their students' learning-problems. For, they had faced more or less the similar kind. So, therefore, it is easier for them to clarify.

Being a linguist, Krashen enunciated principles on how to acquire language in general. He says, 'In the real world, conversations with sympathetic native speakers who are willing to help the acquirer understand are very helpful.'[12] This applies to English learners also. Interested learners of English, be it from high school or college, could interact with native English speakers in this internet age. There are also international institutions for this specific purpose. In the earlier bygone age, India had only English teachers to impart English knowledge by way of grammar and literary text. At present, English language and communication is freely available from many sources, nonetheless, school teachers give a basic foundation.

---

1. John Lyons, Introduction To Theoretical Linguistics, Cambridge University Press 1968 p.177

2. Ibid. p.177

3. Ibid. p.177

4. Ibid. p.178

5. Widdowson, 1989

6. https://www.timesnownews.com/amp/the-buzz/article/votes-cant-be-cast-after-poles-are-closed-donald-trump-trolled-for-misspelling-polls/677182

7. J.J. Gumperz (1970), Sociolinguistics and Communication in small Groups, Sociolinguistics, Selected Readings, Edited by J.B. Pride and Janet Holmes, Penguin Books Ltd, 1972 p.203

8. Schütz, Ricardo E. "Stephen Krashen's Theory of Second Language Acquisition"

9. https://www.sk.com.br/sk-krash-english.html

10. Ibid

11. Ibid

12. Ibid

Chapter-6

Language is for Self-expression

Referring to the English grammar, how complex it is, there is an analogy. If we draw the attention of a centipede that is moving to stop, to ask, as to which leg, he (the centipede) moves first for its locomotion, he becomes too preoccupied with how he did it, he stops moving at all. Similarly, the skills of grammar in English. If we become too self-conscious about how we use language we shall never do it properly again. By citing the example, Randolph Quirk in his book: The Use Of English, writes not to press the analogy of the centipede too far.

'There are many differences between walking and talking, when we walk no one else needs to be involved…walking is a private activity … we do not depend on other people's approval, co-operation, or indeed presence. But talking … the use of language … is social; it depends for its success on doing something not merely as we ourselves like to do it, but in such a way that will fit in with what other people like (or expect or understand).'[1]

Native speakers need not learn grammar explicitly, is the opinion of many. Many in our home or our neighbourhood, do they know the grammar of the language they speak daily? No. For, in all Indian languages that Indians speak, very few learn the grammar of the language formally. But when taught in school, the grammar of the language they speak, they can easily understand. Of course, the rules of the grammar and the labels are difficult to remember and apply. However, since they have a tacit understanding of language and also the language in which it is taught, the task of understanding is much simpler than it is for the English language. Hence, it could be easily concluded that in one's own mother tongue, explicit knowledge of grammar is not considered as a precondition to communicate for speaking or writing. Then, why is grammar taught in the curriculum for native speakers of Hindi, Tamil, Malayalam and other Indian languages in schools? Mainly grammar is taught to enhance or sharpen the writing skills of a student. The written language needs elucidation. The child needs to provide context through illustrations and descriptions in his writings.

For any child to write something basic in his mother tongue is not a problem. This most students can do, what they cannot do is to write well or effectively or impressively, presenting all the views in mind. So, the L 1, teachers seek effectiveness. For an English teacher (of L2/L3) to expect from students both: basic-writing in English and advanced skills of writing, is a far-fetched dream. Because most of the students lack the grammatical skills to write in English. Many academicians argue that writing is a communicative act, in mother tongue grammar teaching is not necessary to communicate. So does, in English. After all, writing is not meant to exhibit grammatical learning items. On the other hand, it is meant for constructions of sentences with appropriate word order and embellishment that enhances the power of communication. That is all latently promoted by grammar.

"Knowledge of language" and "knowledge about language" are two separate things. Many people can speak English but they may not have the knowledge about the language. Only English language teachers impart knowledge about the English language. Here, knowledge about the language means the grammar of the language. For first language learners and native speakers, the grammar may follow automatically. With regard to the second/third language learners of English, explicit teaching of grammar is necessary.

The use of grammar and to form grammatically correct sentences is a part of good education. The importance of grammar was recognised in the English-speaking countries like the U.K and U.S.A in their school curriculum. There was an article that was published in The Baltimore Sun (Nov. 21, 2004) highlighting the importance of grammar at school-level. It also makes a mention of how the English teachers were dusting off their grammar books as part of the school system's effort to bolster students' writing and reading skills. They also regretted that for nearly four decades, grammar instruction was discouraged in schools across the nation (the U.S.A) …But in a back-to-basics move, school officials were emphasizing the need for students to learn grammar as the key to developing strong writing skills. They opined that all students needed to have the type of skills for written communication. To them, if students had poor grammatical skills on resumes or applications, people would judge them as lacking intelligence.[2]

Unfortunately, what they stated is the reality everywhere. Grammatically correct writing is essential to student-success in school and in the workplace. All over the world, from the mid-1980s, grammar instruction has been discouraged in the English teaching pedagogy. Now, many countries are retreating from that position. In the U.S.A, when they implemented the federal No Child Left Behind Act, then their emphasis was laid on testing assessments to measure achievements. That has become the reason for the resurgence of grammar instruction. For better communication, for a wide variety of audiences, while speaking or writing, grammar is essential. People do judge a person by the way he or she communicates. If that was the thinking in a developed English-speaking country, Indians need to take a cue from it seriously. According to the American National Council of Teachers of English (NCTE) – 2008's … 'Writing Now' policy report, it said that their research showed that explicit teaching of grammar, using a context-based functional approach (which focuses on how words, phrases, and sentences work together to make meaning), could help basic writers and English-language learners, improve their writing. It also stated, Grammar, punctuation, and spelling play an important role in the relationship between writers and readers. For, 'Readers expect to see words spelled in a standardized way, for punctuation to be used in predictable ways, for usage and syntax to match…'[3] Even if the teacher teaches all aspects of grammar and writing systematically, students cannot absorb fully. Even by reading books, it cannot happen. Hence, there is a necessity to teach English grammar through daily life situations to students. Of course, there are exceptions. Some students do not require formal grammar teaching, without which they could reach high levels in their second language.

Apart from learning grammar, there are so many other psychological hurdles for students to acquire English as a second language. All said, let us focus on the method of teaching. The latest methods of teaching English focus on communicative approach. In that case, how can questions in the examination always be form-focussed? All the same, in all competitive examinations, the objective questions ask for minute details of formal grammar and structure. Communicative approach originated in English native speaking countries to teach native speakers, obviously fluent in that language. The same cannot be applied to non-natives, when they do not have an English ecosystem.

Generally, English teachers are exposed to various views and ideas, in the field of language learning and speaking. They attend many orientation programmes and read articles. English teachers in particular have a dilemma on how to go about in the class. That is, they have no fixed theory or paradigm, which is never changing in language-teaching. Different ESL teachers use different methods. Method-1 followed by a teacher, can in no way contradict, method-2 followed by another teacher. For, method-1 may yield great results but method-2 may also give relatively the same result. It is the teacher in the class who follows which method suits her students. She, in her wisdom, can also develop a new method after various experiments.

Many teachers cite insufficient exposure to the English language being the biggest reason for not acquiring language. In any English textbook, the exercises based on the grammatical items, are of five or ten sentences. Teachers may provide extra. However, it is better, if students play a participatory role in making them. But it is a huge task. For, students do not come out with their own sentences easily. The biggest hitch is the language-barrier. Moreover, there are many kinds of grammar items in the text-book. Finally, they carry only a single mark. So, therefore, many ESL learners show laxity. 'Languages are complicated. There are hundreds of thousands of words to learn. Dozens, if not hundreds, of grammar patterns to recognize. Conjugation tables to assimilate. Cases to learn to use at the right time…By exposing yourself to the language over a long time, you become a master at recognizing patterns',[4] writes Mathias Barra in medium.com. (Nowadays, many bloggers are airing their experience and opinion on language acquisition). Usually, in the examinations, reading passages are given to comprehend. The questions below are mostly objective types containing some questions on grammar. Barring a few intelligent ones, many cannot answer. Certainly, the method and purpose behind teaching and learning has to be assessed realistically.

The present communicative teaching method of English pays less attention to grammar (unless the context demands for the explanation). This may not work well with the ESL learners. Before, the communicative method of teaching English, grammar-translation method and subsequently structural approach were in practice. The transition to structuralism happened, as it was realized that pure grammatical rules in a prescriptive way, would not help in communication i.e. interaction between individuals and for passing on or receiving messages. Anyhow, the communicative approach to a large extent served well with the English medium students, since they are exposed to English language across the curriculum. When it comes to second language English, the handicap of speaking in English is great. In all in-service training programmes of the English language, teachers are asked to concentrate on students' productive skills by making them participate in role-play, simulation and drama etc., where students must see what is appropriate or appropriateness of language use in the opportunities provided. By losing themselves in the task, learners lose inhibitions to use the language, is the assumption. Of course, it has some merit. This is a way of losing fear to talk by immersing in the task given. Let's analyse this acquisition with respect to language acquisition. While role-playing in the class, students hold the text written and read the lines assigned. They cannot make it on their own.

Panini's grammar

For a long time, in India, English Language and English grammar were taken seriously. To the contrary, there are very few researchers in Panini's grammar to present a cohesive linguistic view of the Indian languages. Way back, it was Sir William Jones that contributed more to linguistics by studying Sanskrit and acquiring command over the language. It is wonderful to listen to his praise for Sanskrit. When Sir William Jones addressed the Asiatic Society on February 2nd 1786, he said, 'The Sanskrit language, whatever be its antiquity, is of a wonderful structure; more perfect than Greek, more copious than Latin, and more exquisitely refined than either…so strong indeed, that no philosopher could examine them all three without believing them to have sprung from some common source, which perhaps no longer exists'.[5] Meant to say that as languages, all three are from one source.

Further, many linguists opined that Indian linguistic work was far superior to the western tradition in grammar and the study of speech sounds. Until then in the West, there had been no systematic study of speech sounds i.e. Phonetics. The Indian insights were influential in the stimulation and development of both the theory and practice of phonetics throughout the century. In grammar too the Indian influence was far-reaching; Panini's description of Sanskrit grammar has been acclaimed from the point of view of its exhaustiveness, its internal consistency and its economy of statement, as far superior to any grammar of any language yet written. Cartesian philosophers like Descartes believed that 'human language is free from stimulus control and does not serve a merely communicative function but it is rather an instrument of free expression of thought and appropriate response to new situations'.[6]

---

1. The Use Of English: Randolph Quirk, Orient Longman 1995, publisher pp. 230-31

2. http://www.ed.gov/news/newsletters/extracredit/2004/11/1122.htm

3. NCTE, 2016, Voyages in English Grammar And Writing, K-8, Loyola Press, p.4 www.voyagesinenglish.com

4. www.medium.com

5. Introduction to Linguistics 1988, P.G.C.T. E - C.I.E.F. L (EFLU), Hyderabad. p. 5

6. N. Krishnaswamy 1971, An Introduction to Linguistics for Language Teachers, Somaiya Publications Pvt Ltd, 172, Naigaum Cross Road, Dadar, Bombay-14DD. P.121

Chapter-7

Primary Education in Mother Tongue - Importance

Introducing English subject (as the second language) from class-1 onwards is not a subject matter of discussion anymore in all states in India. However, to have English as a medium of instruction right from primary education in state government run schools, that cater to the poor and downtrodden, is a debatable one. The states have no such ecosystem for English learning to take place. Suppose, a government school child is asked to name ten birds or ten animals or ten flowers or plants, she would immediately name in her mother-tongue. Because they are in the child's lexicon. Children see the flora and fauna around them and talk in their familiar local language. Could they do the same in English? Now, with the newly introduced English medium, they need to relate and learn by rote English words. It is a stress on their mind. What for, all this trouble in their creative young age? Indian languages carry a rich cultural heritage. That has to be passed on to future generations, through sound foundations.

Perhaps that was the reason why the UNESCO also echoed the same sentiment: 'The death of a language leads to the disappearance of many forms of intangible cultural heritage, especially the invaluable heritage of traditions and oral expressions of the community that spoke it – from poems and legends to proverbs and jokes.'[1] Hence, when a language becomes extinct, a rich repository of cultural knowledge and heritage that has been built diligently and sustained passionately by the ancestors of the language community over many years would also become extinct. The community's world-view through their own language is lost. Language nourishes culture, so to save culture, one has to save the local languages, which is indisputable in a multilingual country. To uphold India's soul: culture, regional languages play a big role, as a medium of instruction to schoolchildren and in literary and cultural circles.

However, there is an imminent threat to the Indian languages nowadays. To protect Indian languages has become an imperative. Ken Hale, the noted linguist says, 'When you lose a language, you lose a culture, intellectual wealth, a work of art. It's like dropping a bomb on…Louvre (a magnificent museum)!'[2] Though there is no severe endangerment of Indian regional languages, they are definitely vulnerable to English language invasion. The National Curriculum Framework (NCF) 2005 rightly states on introduction of English (as the second language and medium of instruction), 'English in India is a global language in a multilingual country …The level of introduction of English is now a matter of political response to people's aspirations rather than an academic or feasibility issue, …'.[3]

Globalization and liberalization of market-economy led to the relegation of Indian languages to the second and third positions compared to that of English being the first. It is lamentable that some minor Indian languages like that of tribal ones are disappearing. 'Languages in education reflect the linguistic double divide; private schools are English-medium schools, and public schools are in the medium of the dominant regional languages with English becoming increasingly important in the higher levels of education,'[4] writes Mohanty. Almost all students and parents know the uses of English and how the language enables: be it in the job sphere or in pursuit of higher studies or to work elsewhere abroad. It is needless to mention that for teachers of English in India; their mother tongue is one of the Indian languages. So, therefore, their own English by way of pronunciation, spelling and grammar are at times in question. This being the case, the state governments-run English medium schools are only for name-sake. Most of the private English-medium schools (barring some convents) are not proper English- mediums (in the sense that standards of English are not maintained up to the mark). By studying in them, students would not become well-equipped in English. In fact, they make them ill-equipped. With no proper teachers to teach English, what students learn is faulty English, which is a permanent impairment. Moreover, to learn in a familiar local language, they easily connect to what they are learning. For a primary school entrant, familiarity of language is helpful. For them English needs much time to connect with what they learn.

There is ample research-based evidence to show that a child should first have primary education in mother-tongue. This is for gaining knowledge at the beginning, in their most easily comprehensible local language. English should be taught as a second language. Whatever knowledge a child gains in their mother-tongue is useful in the other language like that of English. The ASER (Annual Status of Education Report) survey report year after year indicates the basic learning levels of schoolchildren are not up to the mark and quality in education is far behind. '… medium of instruction and language learning are also closely tied to one of the key stated goals of NEP 2020 namely, to ensure foundational literacy and numeracy for all children by Grade 5 so that the poor results in ASER reports can be addressed', opines an educationist and policy framer.[5] According to the New Education Policy (NEP) 2020, up to class-V a child should have education in mother-tongue or regional language. And also to effectively promote Indian languages through multilingualism. A child's mother-tongue, which invariably in many children's cases is the regional language, is the familiar language to the child. To study in mother-tongue initially is less-stressful and more to the understanding of the child.

The Global Education Monitoring Report of UNESCO also states, 'Quality education should be delivered in the language spoken at home. However, this minimum standard is not met for hundreds of millions, limiting their ability to develop foundations for learning. By one estimate, as much as 40% of the global population does not have access to an education in a language they speak or understand.'[6] In spite of that, the Andhra Pradesh (A.P) state government as policy brought into force the English medium from primary education onwards. In India education comes under concurrent list i.e. both the central and state-governments have a hold on it, according to the Constitution of India. The A.P. state government says it has introduced English as medium in primary education at the insistence of parents of school going children. English has become an aspirational goal. The A.P. High Court objected. The High Court of A.P, in April 2020, struck down the government order converting the medium of instruction in government schools from Telugu to English from the academic year 2020. The state government has taken the matter to the Supreme Court of India. To this date it is pending in the Court.[7]

This problem of whether to have education in their own country's languages or in English, is prevalent in many countries of the Asian continent. Like in India, the neighbouring Pakistan also has no proper language policy and made many flip-flops. Jinnah's 1948 speech in Dhaka, spoke, '… on the question of a State language for Pakistan. For official use in this (Dhaka) province, the people of the province can choose any language they wish…There can, however, be only one lingua franca, that is, the language for intercommunication between the various provinces of the State, and that language, should be Urdu and cannot be any other'.[8] Nevertheless, Pakistan has also become ambivalent. The dominance of English is taking place in that country more. Speaking on the subject: 'The Politics of Language Choice in Pakistan', Dr (Prof) Shahid Siddique of Pakistan said that there was a need to protect indigenous languages. For, besides identity and culture a language brings a view-point. Having many languages in a country is something to be appreciated, he said. Because, there is beauty in diversity. More languages meant more view-points. When a language dies not a bunch of expressions die but a whole view-point dies. Differentiation is not done on a linguistic basis but only on a political basis. (Further while agreeing to an extent he added) '…The preference for English by people today is for future prospects, as today's world is pragmatic. You must have a reason to learn a language'.[9]

He continued by saying, 'Globalization poses a challenge. The language attitude of many is: English is an elite language and their children should be exposed to that. That is the linguistic capital they take pride in'.[10] While giving attention to pragmatic use of the English language, the Professor adds that one should ensure that their children get adequate exposure to their own mother-tongue. Because that provides them identity and association with their own cultural i.e. with their own roots. A person's mother tongue is the gate to his history. The sum and substance of his talk is: English language has to be learnt for its advantages but not at the cost of native languages.

On National Language

When European states were developing in the fourteenth and fifteenth centuries the development of national languages was a means of government and education development. After the independence from colonial rule India and Pakistan tried to have their own national language and lingua franca. As India and Pakistan are multilingual countries, it became difficult to develop one national language.

Pakistan somehow was successful to have Urdu as the national language but in India Hindi was not fully adopted. Independent India appointed a commission to recommend a language policy. 'In 1948, when the Linguistic Provinces Commission presented its report to the constituent assembly ... One of the recommendations of the commission to achieve this was the adoption of a national language. Jawaharlal Nehru, for instance, in one of his speeches said 'English had done us a lot of good'... But 'no nation can become great on the basis of a foreign language'. Allowing English to dominate, he felt, would create an elite class and separate them from 'a large mass of our people not knowing English'.[11]

Finally, Benedict Anderson, the political scientist and historian says in one of his lectures in Indonesia, '...the underlying belief (of European linguistic nationalism) was that each true nation was marked off by its own peculiar language and literary culture, which together expressed that people's historical genius...Both India and the Philippines have failed—if that is the right word—to create a generally accepted national language. The colonial language—English and American—remains the effective language of the state and of the national elite. A vigorous English language—and nationalist—literary culture exists in both places, and has accommodated itself to no less vigorous Hindi, Bengali, Tamil, Tagalog and Cebuano cultures.'[12] All in all, native languages have a role in promoting culture and identity. They need to be promoted to keep up the people's historical roots.

---

1. UNESCO on-line atlas seeks to save dying languages || UN News

2. https://works.swarthmore.edu/cgi/viewcontent.cgi?article=1049&context=fac- linguistics p.7

3. National Curriculum Framework (NCF) 2005, Publication Department-National Council for Educational Research and Training (N.C.E.R.T), Sri Aurobindo Marg New Delhi -110016, p.38

4. Language Policy and Education 2 in the Indian Subcontinent 3 Ajit K. Mohanty and Minati Panda, Springer International Publishing AG 2016 T.

McCarty, S. May (eds.), Language Policy and Political Issues in Education, Encyclopaedia of Language and Education, DOI 10.1007/978-3-319-02320-5_37-1 pp.6-7

5. https://www.orfonline.org/expert-speak/the-spirit-of-nep-2020-the-hidden-considerations-in-the-medium-of-instruction-debate/

6. If you don't understand, how can you learn? | Global Education Monitoring Report (unesco.org)

7. Andhra Pradesh defends decision to change medium of instruction in government schools to English - Hindustan Times

8. March 24, 1948 that Jinnah in his speech in the University of Decca. http://www.jinnahofpakistan.com/2010/04/students-role-in-nation-building-24th.html

9. Dr (Prof) Shahid Siddique: https://www.youtube.com/watch?v=ghotOTXsvMs&t=2518

10. Ibid

11. https://www.livemint.com/mint-lounge/features/speaking-in-many-tongues/amp-1560252990853.html

12. https://newleftreview.org/issues/ii9/articles/benedict-anderson-western-nationalism-and-eastern-nationalism

Chapter-8

Preference to English Medium of Instruction-Reasons

In many states of India, parents seek to join their children in English Medium schools. When it comes to the two Telugu-speaking states of Andhra Pradesh (A.P.) and Telangana this is more so. There were raging debates over the medium of instruction 'to be or not to be in English' at the primary level in all state government-run schools. Now it is a settled issue, since both governments of A.P. and Telangana have introduced English Medium right from primary education. All private schools in A. P. and Telangana are of English medium. Even the most down trodden sections of people, be it small land holding peasants, auto-rickshaw drivers, domestic helps, daily-wage workers, fruit and vegetable vendors on the streets, they all spend their hard-earned money to send their children to private English Medium schools nowadays. What for? For the sake of English Medium. Parents' aspiration and desire to enroll their children in the English medium is for job opportunities and a better future. On the other hand, the argument of the A.P. Government was that - English being the lingua franca in a linguistically diverse country India, it (the English language) helps demographically i.e. as a link-language. The state government argued in the apex court: 'India is a country of diversity, and English is essential to enable people to effectively communicate' … defending its decision to convert the medium of instruction in its government schools for all classes/standards … from Telugu to English.[1]

Another Telugu-speaking state, Telangana, is not far behind. Recently (17th Jan 2022) the Telangana cabinet has decided to introduce the English medium in all government schools in the state from the academic year 2022-23. Why? 'The cabinet felt that the parents in rural areas are ready to send their children to the government schools, if the medium of instruction is in English.'[2] Like all market-oriented policies, "English Medium" has become a 'demand and supply' commodity and a politically expedient tool to exploit for political parties. For a long time, in both the states, private English Medium schools mushroomed all over. Of course, to an extent, it is a phenomenon in all states of the country. Because parents trust private management that makes strict rules for teachers against teacher absenteeism and for maintaining punctuality. The private management ensures children's safety and conducts regular assignments followed by immediate feedback (of marks). They also conduct parent-teacher meets, wherein they detail parents on their wards' performance. A kind of performance appraisal of teachers is maintained by them. Above all, the medium of instruction is in English. This gives an edge to the parents. As a consequence, Telugu language is becoming a smaller language in both private and government-run school systems in comparison to the bigger, more dominant and prestigious English. Though linguistically a sad state of affairs, one has to reckon with it.

Why are the underprivileged sections latching on to English for their child's progress? Why can't they get the same progress with regional mediums, where the student's mother tongue plays a big role in understanding the subject knowledge taught? Why are the private English medium students grabbing the limelight, which the government mother tongue or regional medium students are unable to? For a long time these issues of private vs government schools were discussed. The pay to government teachers is more than that of private teachers and they promptly get on the first day of every month their salary unlike most of the private ones. The government teachers are more qualified and would obtain jobs through many screenings like: to get through teacher eligibility test (TET), District Selection Commission (DSC) tests that Directorate of School Education conducts in each state (perhaps testing pattern and nomenclature may differ from state to state), and also viva voce interviews etc. In government schools proper trained teachers teach all subjects. Yet, the schools are unattractive compared to private schools. After a lot of mulling, the state-governments realized the lacunae and tightened the loopholes. They introduced what the parents wanted: the English Medium. Accordingly, the infrastructural facilities are on par with that of private schools. This has improved the enrolment in Andhra and Telangana states. Apart from that, due to Covid-19 Pandemic and persistent lockdowns, the poor became poorer. Economy took a downturn. The only messiah was the government. The enrolment in government schools had risen like never before. One attraction for the poor was and is the English medium, the other being the mid-day meal and snacks provided in the government-school, which is not the case in private schools. Since the government schools do not charge fee, parents are burden-free. This is one good outcome of post-Covid-19 scenario.

The major change in the increase of enrolment in government schools is not derived from some anecdotal references. But it has valid statistical data to back. It is evidently put in the Annual Status of Education Report (ASER 2021). The report says, 'There is a big jump in government school enrolment accompanied by a fall in private school enrolment. The increase in government school enrolment is across the board -- all age-groups, grades and for both boys and girls, … The proportion of boys enrolled in government schools has also increased … narrowing the gender gap.'[3] Earlier it was only the girl-child that was sent to fee-free government schools, as she was supposed to be the liability to parents. Boys were sent to private schools by paying fee to have a bright future. Private schools are supposed to be the standard ones. Now, with the pandemic associated with economic distress, the scenario changed for all.

In a democracy, politicians go by what the people want, rather than, whether it is academically feasible. As stated earlier, the NCF 2005 also states: …'The level of introduction of English is … political response to people's aspirations …'[4] Many argue, countries like China and Russia have scientifically and technologically advanced although they had their native language as a medium of instruction in schools. The reason is not entirely the English education being imparted or not, but how China has placed more emphasis on early education in that country than India did. The Chinese authoritarian form of government has allowed for quicker progress. India also has its advantages of being a democracy but the country recognised very late that it had not invested much in its primary education i.e. the foundational education, where a child develops much. In the New Education Policy (NEP) 2020, all Government Schools will have pre-primary education. It is a reform that has been brought in.

Debates over introduction of English

Soon after getting Independence, the Indian nationalist freedom fighters that formed successive governments wanted to promote all Indian languages. Before the independence, 'although the Orientalists and the Anglicists continued to wrangle, (on the introduction of English language), it was clear the former were steadily losing ground; and Macaulay's celebrated Minute clinched the issue at last. He declared that it was both necessary and possible 'to make natives of this country good English scholars and that to this end our efforts ought to be directed.' The die was cast, and on 7 March 1835, Lord William Bentinck resolved that 'the great object of the British Government ought to be the promotion of European literature and science among the natives of India, and all funds appropriated for the purpose of education would be best employed on English education alone,'[5] writes Prof. M.M. Bhattacharjee.

In the British Raj there were limited people who got educated in the English Convents, purely established in the lines of Babington Macaulay (famous for Macaulay's Minutes of Education 1831) to serve the English and be a legion between the uneducated Indians and colonial masters. The British left, but the English educated dominated the ruling, so therefore, English became an elite language and a language that holds command. After independence many states adopted the local vernacular language as the medium of instruction. Other linguistic minorities residing in those states also obtained their share of propagating their languages by establishing schools either funded or aided by the government or approved by the government. Thus, there was a huge amount of encouragement to Indian languages. There was a fervour of nationalism and patriotism in India that was riding high. However, as usual, the English Convent schools promoted by the British for their benefit continued existing and producing English-speaking graduates. Like earlier, clerical and bureaucratic circles, they played a role disproportionate to the vernacular graduates. The English-speaking people have been getting the edge over others, for being fluent in their speaking, reading and writing of English vis-à-vis the vernacular educated. As a consequence, their domination prevailed. Later, the importance of English grew slowly and steadily leading to a kind of divide in the society between: English-speaking and non-English-speaking. People started treating the English-speaking as elite. There is another reason for this: mostly these English-speaking people come from affluent families. For their affordability, the elite send their children to private convent schools. And also supplement the lacunae in their education by engaging private tuitions or the parental explanations of the lessons and input. Thus, in all ways, the rich and upper middle-class are at an advantage.

So, therefore, the poorer and the disadvantaged sections took to recourse in the government schools. This being the case, the disparity in the society increased many folds. It is not the fault of the government either. They have no escape route. Education, especially primary education, comes under the concurrent list in the Constitution of India. Both the Centre and the States provide syllabi and textbooks to their government run and monitored schools and also to the private schools at the high school level. Hence, the syllabus is uniform for all categories of students. It has no discretion. If uniformity of syllabus is maintained throughout the country, where does the fault lie? Why is there inequality in the society on educational grounds? 'Years ago, noticing the widening social gap between the affordable and unaffordable sections, the Kothari Commission (1964-66), recommended a "common school system" based on the concept of a neighbourhood school. However, that was not implemented in true spirit leading to the present situation. The most technologically and scientifically successful countries in the world like: Russia, Japan, and Germany have a common school system. For them, their state funds the common schools. They promote their language patriotically. They did not need English for higher education. Their entire education including the research-studies are done in mother-tongue. The same is echoed by Prof RK Agnihotri in his report[6] The gulf between the elite and the marginalized sections of society in India is consistently widening, partly due to the way we have organized our school system and the teaching of English. One of the reasons, as already stated, in India there is no common school system. The other is, teaching of English in elite convents is different compared to non-elite schools.

In India the dichotomy in school systems is causing schism. The usual and oft-repeated complaint about the government schools is: there is 'no quality in education' in them. People cite two main reasons for this condition. One, government teachers are often sent on Census and Electoral Duties and other duties affecting the regular routine of teaching at school. Two, the absenteeism of government teachers is more to schools. Government teachers have more casual and medical leave compared to private school teachers. The substitution in their absence should compensate for the loss. However, practically that is not always possible. In private schools, due to paucity of leave, absenteeism by teachers to a large extent is absent. Teacher's regularity propels educational outcomes among students. Because of which, the thread of teaching would not be lost. Like how student's absenteeism costs dearly to a student with raising gaps in knowledge, teacher absenteeism would also affect the teaching-learning process. Students get used to a particular teacher teaching the subject. Their mind gets tuned to it. Suddenly, with a substitute teacher they cannot get attuned so easily.

We are aware that the government teachers in all states of India are selected through a thorough testing and screening. They are more often highly qualified than the private teachers. The kind of mathematics and science teachers one finds in government schools are not found in private schools. However, English teachers are supposed to be good in private schools/convents. That is also one of the reasons why the poor join their children in private schools. Government agencies lay down the curriculum after well-thought-out programmes. This curriculum applies to all the schools in the same way. Like in private schools, the Government schools also provide additional present-day technological aids: T.V; Computers along with the internet, but only to a small number of high schools. In all these infrastructural and technological spheres private institutions are well in advance. They collect money from parents for providing these facilities, while collecting fee for the student. As a matter of fact, there is a lot of gradation in private English medium schools right from the fee-structure to standards in teaching. So is their teaching-learning process. Elite in India send to top most schools, the upper middle classes to high fee private schools, then the middle and lower middle that includes the poor according to their affordability, relatively less fee charging ones. These are all English medium schools! Some say the so-called less fee charging private English-medium schools are not necessarily good at teaching English. They are a kind of non- standard-English mediums. The most abandoned ones right now are the government schools in most of the states of India. Many are dilapidated with no proper infrastructure and no proper staff in remote areas. Of course, the state governments are cognisant of this fact and are trying to improve. As enunciated earlier, Covid-19 Pandemic and the economic distress caused the poor to join their children in government schools. In any case, the state-governments in all the states in India are making their schools more attractive to get enrolment. Delhi government schools have become role-models with innovative programmes.

There is another aspect to be noticed. That is monolingual English classrooms and also English is the only language in school. All over India, English medium schools give prominence to English, leaving students' mother tongue or local language in lurch. It is said, some of the schools punish their students for speaking in local language on the school premises. As a result, they have very little knowledge in their local language that is most often their mother tongue. Apart from that, being in the English Medium, mostly they look down upon their mother tongue. To put it candidly, often the teacher that teaches their mother tongue would not get due regard for teaching it in those schools. The students take little light of their L1 teacher and what she teaches. Usually, L1 teachers in English medium schools get hurt because of jokes or puns made on them. This culture has to change. The NCF 2005 states '…in "English-medium" schools, where children's other Indian languages need to be valorised to reduce the perceived hegemony of English.'[7] But, that is not happening on the ground. Occasionally, regional vernacular medium students assemble in campuses with the English medium ones for competitive examinations and sports. It is the perception of many vernaculars that English medium teachers and students behave as if they were the privileged ones. They as a whole shun to speak the local language making the vernaculars guilty. In this pathetic scenario, encouraging multilingualism in all schools becomes a welcome change.

As a matter of fact, English is a popular language by historical accident rather than its linguistic superiority. No language is superior or inferior to any other language.'- This statement that comes out from linguists, although true, at the grassroot level, the situation is different in India. In an article, Mohan Guruswamy, the renowned public intellectual writes that English is the language of the affluent elite in India and that elite looks down upon the vernaculars. He also states, 'People, who go to elite schools or even good English medium schools catering to the wealthy and well-connected, speak English with the regional accents ironed out of it. They are fluent in it and look down on others with condescension… they are called "vernacs"'.[8] Even if this is considered as his personal opinion, in an opinion piece of a national English newspaper, there appears to be some truth in it. In any case, his opinion is the opinion of many people, who studied in the vernacular medium in India.

Reasons for parents opting for English medium to their children

Good or bad, parents in many parts of India, view English language as an enabler and is perceived to blur the divide between the rich and the poor, with the fruits of English education they could develop to fill the gap of economic inequality. And also, many opine, English being a link language, it brings unity in diversity. In this digital age, English is the language for employment opportunities within India and abroad, as it is the international language. However, the dreams of this section have many constraints to get fulfilled. Initially the government schools were unwilling to introduce English education in schools, as they perceived it impracticable. Moreover, many academicians speculated the feasibility of a child learning knowledge in an unfamiliar language at an early age. As the demand grew for the English medium, the private English medium schools started mushrooming all over. It's always the tendency of the parents to give what they were deprived of to their children. From the poorer sections also, people have seen the advantage of having a small family. They are striving to send children to private schools, as they have developed trust-deficit in government school education. This has many reasons. Some of them were cited earlier. Surprisingly, most of the government school teachers, sending their children to private English-medium schools, instead of joining their own, tells the tale. The Position Paper of English (NCF 2005) states, 'English in India today is a symbol of people's aspiration and their fuller participation in national and international life and its colonial origins now forgotten or irrelevant'.[9]

Earlier, the English language was thought to be a colonial legacy and was a burden to carry. There was also a view that it colonized Indian minds. And it (English language) represents English culture. Now, these theories fizzled out, as more and more opted for learning English, as they found it to be an enabler in furthering their talents, be it in education or in outside pursuits of business. Now, the English language is more utilitarian than cultural. In India, except for some highly educated literary figures, European literature would not gain ground.

Long ago, a famous Telugu newspaper editor, who was very good in the English language, when asked, as to which language he preferred writing in? He said wittily, 'writing books and articles in Telugu is like acting in dramas (acting in theatre is somewhat a down-graded thing compared to acting in movies in India) but writing the same in English, is like acting in cinemas. Of course, there is wide readership for the vernacular newspapers but they are limited to their own state's jurisdiction. Unlike English newspapers, the ideas would not spread all over the educated sections. In the psyche of Indians, English is assuming a higher position vis-à-vis the Indian language. People think their voice would be heard nationally and internationally, if they had knowledge in English. As a result of this, there is slow death of Indian languages. For instance, if a Telugu child is asked to say, what the Telugu word equivalent for light or heat, he or she cannot say in these days. Similarly, if asked what the green colouring substance chlorophyll of a leaf or the starch in a plant are called in their local language or mother-tongue, they do not have an answer. For, they do not have in their repertoire of vocabulary what to say in Telugu, as they switched over to the English medium. Of course, one good thing with them is, they understand their science textbook (written in English), not through English to English, but through Telugu/vernacular to English in their minds, invariably using English technical terms. This kind of retention of vernacular language is appreciable but not adequate enough to promote or sustain the language in the coming years.

Even students thinking in their mother tongue has its own limitations. With limited thought processes in English, they rely mostly on their mother tongue for cognitive understanding. Perhaps, this would not help students in expressing themselves in higher scientific forums at the university level. Of course, there are very few people who reach that stage of education eventually. Basically, many are confined to limited purposes of doing routine jobs, after a certain qualification. David Graddol in one of his main conclusions, after examining the complex nature of English in India (both in education and employment sectors) writes, 'Indian universities fall far short of rival countries in the quality of their teaching, research, and graduates. Poor English skills is one of the causes.'[10] So, therefore, to be able to express themselves, the students are encouraged by their English teachers to think deliberately in English. This deliberate thinking helps them to explore their strengths and weaknesses in English language and free flow of thought. They could rectify their linguistic handicaps either by themselves by referring to books or by seeking the experts' opinions. After all, to be well-equipped in English need not necessarily lead to being ill-equipped in mother-tongue or local language. One language complements the other, if handled side-by-side. In this aspect the NCF 2005 Position Paper for English says: 'English does not stand alone. The aim of English teaching is the creation of multilinguals who can enrich all our languages...'[11] seems to be sound.

Many Asian countries have had a colonial past. Majority of them were all ruled by the British. However, all countries adopted their mother tongue as a national language and also as language for imparting education. China, Japan, Korea, Thailand, Malaysia and others adopted their own state languages. The only two eastern nations that went for English are Philippines and India because of uncertainty in deciding which way to go',[12] said Benedict Anderson, the noted political scientist and historian in his talk in Indonesia. (on "Western Nationalism And Eastern Nationalism- Is there difference that matters?") He further adds, 'Both India and Philippines have failed... if that is the right word ... to create a generally accepted national language. The colonial language ... English (in India) and American (in Philippines) ... remains the effective language of the state and of the national elite.'[13]

That being the case in India, interestingly, Dr Shahid Siddiqui, (the renowned linguist and educationist of Pakistan), responded to a question, when asked ... on parents giving prominence to English in Pakistan, instead of their mother tongue in Urban houses, he said, 'Parents want their children to be exposed to the English language because they take pride in that linguistic capital, which they think is beneficial and important for their future prospects.'[14] Yet, he cautioned not to lose sight of the mother tongue that gives them their child's identity, cultural and historical perspectives. Nevertheless, when people started making their choice for want of English medium schooling, mother tongue education has automatically started taking the back-seat. No one thinks this trend is ominous. Hence, the crucial dilemma is how to protect native languages, while enhancing English language capabilities? This plight is in the minds of all nationalist thinkers.

---

1. https://www.hindustantimes.com/andhra-pradesh/andhra-pradesh-defends-decision-to-change-medium-of-instruction-in-government-schools-to-english/story-1dDAQxyXHqOtqtTi1XgzfN.html

2. All Telangana govt schools to become English medium from next academic year | Education News, The Indian Express

3. https://www.deccanchronicle.com/opinion/columnists/301121/rukmini-banerji-and-wilima-wadhwa-covid-effect-changes-in-schooling.html

4. National Curriculum Framework (NCF) 2005, Publication Department-National Council for Educational Research and Training (N.C.E.R.T), Sri Aurobindo Marg New Delhi -110016, p.38

5. KR Srinivasa Iyengar 1995, Introduction, Indian Writing in English, Sterling Publishers Pvt. Ltd., New Delhi-110016 (Bengal: Past and Present, No.134, 1953) (p.27) [xa1]

6. https://www.academia.edu/5905884/Multilingualaity_and_the_teaching_of_English_in_India?email_work_card=view-paper

7. National Curriculum Framework (NCF) 2005, Publication Department-National Council for Educational Research and Training (N.C.E.R.T), Sri Aurobindo Marg New Delhi -110016, p.39

8. https://www.nationalheraldindia.com/amp/story/opinion%2Fwhat-makes-the-elite-think-they-are-smarter

9. NCF 2005 English Position Paper 1.4 NCF English Position Paper.pdf p.1

10. David Graddol: English Next India, British Council 2010, p.15

11. National Curriculum Framework (NCF) 2005, Publication Department, National Council for Educational Research and Training (N.C.E.R.T), Sri Aurobindo Marg New Delhi -110016, p.39

12. https://newleftreview.org/II/9/benedict-anderson-western-nationalism-and-eastern-nationalism

13. Ibid

14. https://www.youtube.com/watch?v=ghotOTXsvMs&t=2518s

Chapter-9

Introduction of English Medium-Opposing views

Historical reason for English domination

For years on end, English dominated Indian society. It's considered as a language that has been associated with sophistication and decency. The prime reason being connected with English mannerism. Again, the good manners like greeting someone: good morning, good afternoon, good day etc. apart from that the mannerisms like saying: please, sorry, excuse me etc. are part and parcel of the English acquired by Indians from the colonial era. Above all, the English people taught Victorian morals, which Indians also have the equivalents of their own. The Indian Constitution is based on the western English code or values adopted by Indians. Due to the colonial influence, the renaissance that had taken place in Italy, the Reformation movement that questioned the church in the West leading to critical thinking and the spirit of enquiry, supported by Indian ethos, took a shape in Indian education. To top it all, the English educated had a say, all the time. By taking cognisance of the prevailing situation, the middle classes who had been confined to mother-tongue or local language medium, hitherto, have been slowly shifted to the private English medium schools, bidding adieu to the public government schools.

After independence, for a long time, only public i.e. government - run schools imparted education to all sections of people. Then, there was equity in education. As far as access is concerned, the British ensured the establishment of neighbourhood schools even in India following their reformation principles. With the opening up of the economy, the lower middle classes became affluent and moved up the ladder. They not only joined their children in English medium but also filled the lacunae and strengthened the capacity to increase their child's understanding and subject knowledge in English, by way of tuition. Ultimately, the government run public schools have become the bastions of the poor and uncared. The most surprising part of the public or government-run schools is, as stated earlier, the teachers working in those schools also send their children to the private English medium schools!

Generally, students studying in English medium schools' fare better in English than those studying in the local language medium. That is the reason why many students opt for English medium. The language learnt from the beginning is different from the language learnt later in life. The language acquisition along with right pronunciation takes place in early childhood. The language English learnt later in life has a tinge of contrived artificiality. If English is purely learnt as a language in the non-English medium school, the exposure to the language by way of listening, speaking, reading and writing is less compared to English-medium students. However, for the first-generation learners of English, teaching non-trivial (deep and serious) concepts cannot be understood in English. Hence, there is a need for primary classes up to class-v, to be taught in mother tongue/regional medium. Of late, the poorer strata among the society are also seeking English for their children as a medium of instruction. To them, their emancipation would be by the upward mobility for which English is a catalyst to catapult.

The types of English-medium schools

As discussed earlier, the middle and the upper middle classes have a series of private English medium schools with different fee-structure. Those that could afford more, would send their children to somewhat a standard school. The others, based on their affordability, send to the other lesser private schools. Somehow, these low-graded private schools, outwardly English medium to attract the middle class, are not truly so. Finally, the poor are taught in government schools in their mother tongue or regional language medium. Pointing out this disparity, a Dalit professor writes, '… most of the upper castes opt for good private English Medium schools, whereas the poor rural lower caste ones are left to Government Mother Tongue medium schools, which defies the principle of "equality"'.[1] If they seek the English medium and opt out from government schools, the government has a problem. It has to wind up some of its schools. Of course, this has been the case in South Indian Telugu-speaking states now. If the government shifts to the English medium, it could, to an extent, contain the exodus, is the idea. After all, the government is in the education field only to socially uplift the poor. When the poor desert it, it has to close down all its schools. Most of the state governments have nearly sixty percent of state employees from the education sector. It creates jobs for so many. But the poor think that their upward mobility is in English education. In both southern states of Andhra Pradesh and Telangana, parents from the lower economic strata have selected English as their medium. Consequently, the strength of the government schools has fallen down. This led to the almost closing down of some schools. In some other schools the number of teachers exceeded the number of students. In that case, salaries are paid without taking work by the government. However, there is a counter argument from the leftists in Kerala state, the state government schools impart best of the education in Malayalam medium and therefore, those who migrated to private English medium school are reverse migrating. Possibly, there is truth in it. Because, students understand in their mother tongue more than in any other language, especially not so in English. Personal experiences made some students take this reverse gear to their mother tongue for their benefit. This choice of medium should be left to parents, so that they decide what suits their child. Or otherwise, parents should be educated on the benefits of teaching in their mother tongue up to primary level and how important it is for their children to have so.

The manner in which the private English-medium schools are rapidly spreading, is amazing. They are competing with the neighbouring government schools rather than among themselves. As a matter of fact, they are not English medium schools in the proper sense. They are English mediums only for name-sake. For, most of them do not provide good English teachers, in the sense, to teach science, mathematics and social sciences in English. The English teachers appointed are somewhat competent in teaching English, but not the other subject-teachers viz. mathematics, science and social studies, that are taught in English in English medium schools. When other subjects are taught with faulty pronunciation and grammar, a student is likely acquiring the same. In this regard, the teacher of English in English medium schools is helpless. In a way, mother tongue/regional medium schools are better. For, the teacher of English in these schools is the exclusive subject-expert and authority.

The premise on which the advocates of mother tongue/regional language medium argue is:

i. Linguistic or emotional interaction is the foundation for mother tongue. The dominant discourse of the second language (English) never acknowledges this.

Nonetheless, on the ground, people moved away from this premise. When the elite of India deliberately embraced English and English as a medium of instruction, none of those arguments applied, is the point. The divide in the society paved the way for the choice for English. The people at the lower strata i.e. the Dalits are asking for it. They have built a temple for English. Depending on the socio-economic conditions, India is different to different sections. From the beginning, the elite upper classes of the society are sending their children to standard convents, where English is the medium of instruction. The children of the elite cope with it because they live in those environs i.e. at home English seems to be their mother tongue and their own heritage language, the other tongue. Knowing the benefits of the language, BR Ambedkar called English: the "milk of the lioness" that will help Dalits roar.[2]

However, for many years politicians in various states, especially in Hindi heartland opposed the introduction of English as ESL from class-1 onwards. They were under the impression that their act of opposing would connect with people at the lower rung of society. Initially, it did, but later it did not. Finally, Dalits started clamouring for English-medium education. This, David Graddol has succinctly put it in his book, by writing … The Dalit movements demand for English is part of a wider desire … But the politics around English have shifted in the last decade, where populist politicians once secured rural votes by promising to banish English, now there is a powerful grass-root lobby to extend English to the masses.'[3]

ii. English can be studied as a language in the best possible way by hiring the best and expert teachers. After all, you want the language. That can be achieved without being in the English medium,

It is the call for encouraging non-English medium students to remain in their place. Anyhow, that call is hollow, as far as fluency in English is concerned. Let me flip the coin and speak. Those who study in their mother tongue medium are fluent in their mother tongue in listening, speaking, reading and writing. Their English knowledge happens to be, as much as, or little lesser or slightly more than the input given by the teacher. It becomes greater when they enhance the skills of English by extra reading or supplementary reading they do outside. This has been put in a nutshell by NCF 2005 in this paragraph: 'The relative success of "English medium" schools shows that language is learnt when it is not being taught as language, … We should in this way move towards a common school system that does not make a distinction between "teaching a language" and "using a language as a medium of instruction'.[4]

Hence, an input-rich environment is necessary to learn any language, be it first language. Suppose a student studies in mother tongue or regional language medium school, his regional language capacity increases manifold. For he grasps regional language terminology of science words, social sciences, mathematics and environment. Nobody needs to give meaning, when he learns a new word in any subject. Whereas the English medium teacher has to make them understand or provide a mother tongue equivalent. However, the context provides meaning, but it is not always correct. The formal regional/local words for: solution, solvent, catalyst, equation, triangle, rectangle, fence, field are known for a local medium student in his regional/local language. But not known to an English medium student. When all are opting for English medium, this rich repertoire of local native languages' vocabulary will go down the history, confining to compendiums. A sad state of affairs for Indian languages!

In any case, can we attribute India's success in Information Technology (IT) to English? undoubtedly yes. But some cynics say:

iii.　'… the idea that India's software success is due to the knowledge of English bears examining. If it were true, then English speaking countries must display this advantage consistently'.[5]

Indeed, India's success in software is due to the knowledge in English. But that itself is not sufficient. There are people with scant spoken English, who could do well in software, as they have expertise in technical knowledge. Strangely, some could read and comprehend the technology written in English, but were unable to express it orally in English language. undoubtedly, knowledge in English helps technicians to express themselves and their work-done. When they need to communicate how they were able to do, so and so program successfully, English fluency helps. Because, they are talking to their peer-groups and their bosses, who are English-speaking most often. For communication, one needs abundant language skills and articulation. More than fluency, to talk in English language, what some software professionals need to know is appropriateness. The vocabulary, the mannerism in which they speak and explain things is much more important. In recent times, Infosys Founder Narayana Murthy also mentioned the need for English in the job market, especially in Software. He says, 'Whether we like it or not, the only official link language for the college-educated people in India is English. I know several youngsters… who have completed their degrees in vernacular, but were forced to take up jobs at a much lower level than they deserve, due to their inability to speak English reasonably fluently…'[6]

Of late, in other countries of Asia, the demand for English is increasing. Especially, to talk to and exchange opinions among themselves. 'A 2017 report pointed out that China now leads the world for the number of English-medium international schools, with over 800 of them. And that market continues to grow: Studies have found that the demand for English education is high…'[7] In any case, there are also some expert-educationists in India, who are doubtful of the wisdom of imparting education in a student's mother-tongue or local language. Their apprehension is, in an increasingly connected global society, choosing one's mother tongue over English may not prepare students to face the real world.

What do linguists say about English vis-à-vis the local language?

As per linguistics, spoken language comes first and it is followed by the written. A child's spoken language at home and outside, generally, is the mother-tongue/local language. So, the child understands spoken language at a tender age, then followed by it, later learns how to write and present what he understood. If that be the case, the craving for English medium impairs, partially the mental growth of the child. The child thinks in his own language, not in English, however much he is exposed to English in the school. Of course, in exceptional cases, the educated parents at home give a lot of input in the English language for their child to naturally acquire. As students go to higher classes, the mental strain on them gets reduced because of age and maturity. She or he knows the purpose of learning English and speaking.

There is another theory in support of mother tongue education. These theorists say, mother-tongue is like mother's milk i.e. nourishment for the child's physical and mental growth at initial stages. Any person who is weak in their mother-tongue, is weak in an-other tongue also. Surprisingly, some of the grown-ups, who studied in their mother tongue/regional medium, can read a difficult text in English and write and execute a difficult program on the computer but are unable to express how they had done it in spoken English. Hence, exposure to speaking is a must. English is no more a foreign language in India. It is the second official language after Hindi. Any language is first learnt by listening to it and then speaking it. Hence, there is an advantage for the English medium students, as far as listening to the English language in all subjects and reading the concepts in English, by which, they unconsciously acquire the skills of the language. All in all, the debates and discussion on English do not lead to a final conclusion. The dichotomy between native languages and English, persists.

1. Kancha Illiah https://thewire.in/education/macaulay-english-medium-new-education-policy

2. Sankrant Sanu, The English Medium Myth - Dismantling Barriers to India's Growth — Garuda Prakashan Private Limited, Gurugram, India. p.59

3. English Next India, David Graddol, British Council 2010, p.65

4. National Curriculum Framework (NCF) 2005, Publication Department-National Council for Educational Research and Training (N.C.E.R.T), Sri Aurobindo Marg New Delhi -110016, p.39

5. Sankrant Sanu, The English Medium Myth - Dismantling Barriers to India's Growth, Garuda Prakashan Private Limited, Gurugram, India. p.35

6. https://www.moneycontrol.com/news/business/it-is-time-we-accepted-english-as-an-indian-language-and-encourage-it-as-any-other-indian-language-infosys-founder-narayana-murthy-7227061.html

7. https://www.deccanherald.com/opinion/in-perspective/english-phobia-will-ruin-india-s-economic-prospects-869208.html

Chapter-10

English Second Language Students-Practical Difficulties in Speaking

In June 2016, Alan Maley published an article titled: 'More Research is needed' – A Mantra Too Far?' In which he argued, 'research and the practice of teaching are quite different forms of activity, with no necessary connection between them... We recognise the value and legitimacy of research and theory-building within its own domain. But we should not expect … close link with the activity of teaching.'[1]

Maley has shown the disconnect between the research and what is going on in the teaching-learning within the class. ESL learners make many mistakes while speaking. Because, they are not used to speaking English. The kind of mistakes learners make are unimaginable for researchers or the professors in English academic circles. Teachers do not complain on these issues, because they feel awkward to expose themselves. If done, it bounces back on them and their inability to teach. Ultimately, the blame comes on them, but not on what they are pointing out as a problem area. Here, I would like to provide my personal experience as an English second/third language teacher.

Once (this was in the year 2005), it so happened, I asked my students of class ix (Telugu Medium learners of ESL, with a rural background) to give a 2-minute talk on one of their dearest friends. I even provided simple guidelines for them to speak. I just told them to mention their friend's name first, her likes and dislikes, her habits, and what my student likes in her (physical features as well as attitudes towards things etc.). To me, as their English language teacher, what mattered most was their coming out (leaving inhibitions) and speaking openly than their grammatical accuracy and functional appropriateness. To me it was astonishing to hear their talk and language disabilities in their utterances. It was so alarming, after sometime; I started noting down their sentences to analyse what went wrong in their grammar. Some of the sample sentences of their speech are as follows:

Today, I want to speak about my best friend (provided by me, their teacher).

I am giving here what most of the students made mistakes of. They started off after mentioning the name of the friend, by saying.

1. "She is like subject..."

    (Instead of using the main lexical verb 'like' by saying ''She likes the subject science/social studies/English etc.", they used the auxiliary also along with the lexical verb 'like' that is not required.)

2. "She is voice beautiful."

    (Meaning to say 'she has a beautiful or sweet voice.')

3. "She is favourite colour is pink and green"

    (To say 'her favourite colours are pink and green'.)

4. "She habits is very good."

    (Instead of saying 'she has very good habits.')

    (The above mistakes indicate that students are prone to use 'unnecessary use of auxiliary' and 'lack of knowledge of possessive pronouns').

    Some other students made other kinds of mistakes like:

5. "She is like pink and green."

    (To say 'She likes pink and green (colours).')

6. "She is a very good habits."

    (Instead of 'she has very good habits')

7. "My friend is a like subject English and Mathematics."

    (To say 'my friend likes the subjects: English and Mathematics.)

(The above indicates unnecessary use of articles apart from other mistakes.)

The above sentences were only a few of my observations. Their spoken errors are unending to quote. The most moot question here is … where does the fault lie? Is it because they don't speak English enough? Or they do not get opportunities to speak (in the class or outside)? Or they don't have the intuitive knowledge of grammar to make meaningful sentences? Or are they not exposed to wide reading (to passively absorb the patterns of sentence constructions)? However, as Prabhu, the noted English academician, said this may be like 'Learners' … 'find themselves producing the language before they are ready for it, and make errors by overgeneralization,'[2]

In the communicative approach to teaching English (which is done in classrooms nowadays) grammar or structure of language is taught in a veiled manner i.e. not in an explicit way. The approach focuses more on meaning. Hence, some key elements of formal grammar are neglected. 'Students must understand how language is a structured system before they can understand more functional communicative uses. Language structure is taken for granted by most people,' writes Donald G. Ellis, Professor of Communication at the University of Hartford.[3]

However, in India, right from the beginning i.e. from the pre-primary, structures are drilled. If we open any Lower Kindergarten book, we find: This is a book. - That is a tree. - These are mangoes. - Those are apples. - I like my school. - My school uniform is blue and white etc. A singular noun like: book is preceded by an article – 'a' and the plural noun: mangoes by null (no article). In the same way, lexical verbs have no auxiliaries. Then why are the learners using the extra things that are not grammatically correct to add on? The answer is: they are not used to speaking, so this is fumbling. While writing also regional medium students i.e. ESL ones of rural background, commit the same mistakes, if they are asked to write freely. The memorized text-answers, in most cases, are with correctly formed sentences. In the Communicative approach and in the discourse-oriented pedagogy (followed in A.P. and Telangana), while correcting the answer-scripts writing-mistakes are ignored for want of meaning the students convey. For, the mistakes get set-right, once they move ahead to the next level.

In the primary classes, students are taught to distinguish different initial sounds viz. pin, tin, bin, … mat, rat, cat, etc and suffixes viz. -er, e.g. farm-farmer, drive-driver, teach-teacher etc. meaning dependent words like: a walking stick is not a stick walking: a dining table is not a table dining, a tooth paste is not a paste tooth even though the words are the same. By listening to word-initial and word-final sounds, students learn how the patterns are and how the meaning changes with prefixes and suffixes and how particular order of words convey meaning.

During and after Covid-19, one big change in the education system is digitisation. The learning curve now would be digital. Therefore no dearth for English exposure. Nowadays, high school children are more privileged to see English T.V. Channels of India and the West to acquire proper pronunciation, vocabulary and structure. Moreover, there are English learning apps, online dictionaries on their mobile phones to know the meaning and pronunciation. Further, there are various social media channels, where they can listen to native speakers teaching English. If they have the language aptitude there are umpteen number of possibilities to gain. Now, in the post Covid-19 era, the students are much tech-savvy with their mobile apps and social media outlets. The days of teaching- learning in silos, have vanished. There are many teachers, apart from classroom teacher, and many schools, away from school. However, a physical brick and mortar school and physical touch of a teacher by giving a pat on the back or slight reprimand are never replaceable.

To carry on conversations in ESL

'Language learning evolves out of learning how-to carry-on conversations. One learns how to do conversation, one learns how to interact verbally, and out of this interaction syntactic structures are developed'.[4]

India being a multilingual country, many Indian languages are caught orally by conversations. To learn any language by talking to the native speakers of the language is easy. It is done in a free atmosphere. There are no stringent punishments or threats from outside, because it is a voluntary action. This action is self-driven. Whereas, to learn English in India, no such situation prevails. No English-speaking community around for a learner. In a conditioned classroom, to talk in English is an uphill task for ESL learners. The subject is unknown, the grammar is vast, if at all to learn, the opportunities outside the school are almost nil. Even if learners try to, they are laughed at. Within the school, whatever opportunities are provided by the teacher, they are all contrived and would not lead to real learning.

Even in role-play and pair-drill activities, the learners do parrot-like recitation of the lines given in English in their roles. For instance, once students were asked (by me) to enact roles of Portia, Antonio, Bassanio, Shylock etc. in Shakespeare's drama: 'The Merchant of Venice', on the scene of trial before judgment. Students could not say their dialogues orally. They literally carried script-written and parroted the dialogue by reading it. Usually, students do not have the language for carrying out the conversation. However, ESL learners enjoy reading text by opting to play roles. In a class of forty, five to seven students take the roles and deliver the dialogue seeing the text of a given script. Next five enthusiastically, as another batch, come forward to enact. Though they are not conversant in English language, they are keen on acting and delivering dialogues in English. All in all, there is no dearth of enthusiasm in participating in various activities related to the English language by students. Though there is no enabling environment to acquire the English language, yet, they try to participate in activities. Of course, digital platforms of today are a different ball game. They are useful for advanced learners that could use them.

---

1. Training Language and Culture, Volume 2 Issue 1, 2018, The teacher's sense of plausibility, ALAN MALEY (tlc journal.org) Research Is Needed- A Mantra Too Far- Alan Maley.pdf

2. Ibid p.26

3. G. Ellis is Professor of Communication at the University of Hartford, West Hartford, CT 06117. COMMUNICATION EDUCATION, Volume 42, January 1993 Downloaded by [National Communication Association] at 12:16 10 July 2015) *CommunicationEducationLanguageandCommunication.pdf

4. https://applingtesol.wordpress.com/2018/10/13/do-teacher-trainers-promote-good-practice/ (Hatch 1978, p. 404).

Chapter–11

Bilingualism in ELT

In India, since the states (provincial states) are carved on linguistic basis, English is taught in bilingual method i.e. using the regional language in the English classroom. This is the usual practice in all state government-run schools. Not only in schools, but also in colleges and universities, usually the talk on the subject revolves round in the regional language, though the subject matter is in English. Many academicians of English opposed the use of mother tongue/ regional language in the English classroom, simply, because the target-language i.e. English gets neglected. However, in most of the mother tongue or regional language medium schools, the bilingual method is used in teaching of English, as a common method of practical use. This has many reasons. The easy and simple reason being that it is easy for learners to understand the content given in their own language. If an English class becomes a mother tongue class, it supplements the mother tongue more than the other tongue i.e. English is one argument.

The usual objections cited by a professor in Linguists on the use of the mother tongue in a second language (English) learning situation are:

a)   We will be opening the flood-gates and there will be no end to the use of the mother tongue.

b)   There won't be enough practice in the language that is being taught.

c)   Words in one language do not correspond to words in another.

d)   The description of a language has to be in its own terms and not in terms of another language.[1]

Nevertheless, in many workshops for teachers, it has been pointed out, instead of struggling hard to make students understand something difficult, like say some ad hoc vocabulary items or some abstract poetic lines, the teacher could judiciously use some amount of mother tongue, as and when necessary. But that should be done in a restricted way. Using students' mother tongue or local language to understand certain items of language, eliminates waste of time and makes learning more meaningful. The translation of grammar is in some ways helpful, as it has language universals. Paradoxical as it may seem, Second Language Acquisition (SLA) researchers seem to have neglected the fact that the goal of SLA is bilingualism. UNESCO defines the second language, 'as a language acquired by a person in addition to his mother tongue.[2]

As per English subject experts, the methodology of teaching English is different. The text given in the textbook/course-book is not a lesson to be taught using the bilingual translation method. The text is a 'reading passage' for the learners to read and comprehend. The teacher only facilitates them in comprehending. The teacher's work is to simplify or should elicit what is given in the reading passage by asking questions after the students read. For which, a teacher needs to make the passage into meaningful chunks. In each chunk, the difficult vocabulary items have to be made clear with their meaning, and then leave the students for silent reading to comprehend, followed by questions. There should be thorough grounding of the structure in the passage. Teachers should ask students to make sentences based on the structure, so that they can have a better understanding of using it later. Yet, all these steps are not followed faithfully by many teachers to make the student a main participant in the teaching-learning process. Student-centric method requires a lot of prior preparation on the part of the teacher. The teacher has to thoroughly prepare before taking the class.

To ask direct, simple but to the point questions, is an art on the part of the teacher. Making questions shows the skill of a particular teacher. For, a teacher who lacks much of language competence, labours a lot to frame a question and makes the student's position difficult to answer. For English language students, locative questions starting with what, when or which are easier. Because students could easily locate a historical date or time or place in a given passage. Whereas, the inferential questions, based on between the lines reading, are tougher. Here, they need to properly understand and infer the meaning and convey it in the target language. The toughest part is the evaluative questions that are most often asked with a: why? The student's valued assessment and judgment depend on this type of question. Here, students' critical thinking plays a role. For creativity, open-ended questions are given in all English texts. However, second language learners of English are mostly found tight-lipped to answer them. This is for two reasons. One, in our school system, teacher-teaching and student-listening, is deep-rooted. Critical faculties are rarely tapped, as the teacher is engrossed in completing the syllabus-set for the class, as per the academic calendar. Two, the student's inability to speak or think in English and to answer in English. Last but not the least, the age-old notion … that the teacher is meant to impart wisdom and students to swallow it silently. For generations, the brains stopped there. Bilingual method helps here, in a way, for some students to open up.

This bilingualism was experimented in my class. Often when I said in the class, 'you don't need to give an answer fully in English (for an evaluative and open-ended question), you can use your mother tongue along with English (code-switching) to give the answer'… yet there was no response. It is very difficult to elicit answers in English class. For, students seem to have an understanding that the teacher is all-knowing, knowledgeable. Hence, the teacher has to give the answer, why should we rack our brains? To students, the teacher should do all the thinking and should give whatever they need in mother-tongue or local language. They think that understanding would help them write the examination. My students used to always ask me, 'Please teach the whole lesson in Telugu, we'll understand and answer in the examination.' As if to say, why bother us in between the lesson, with all these comprehension questions in English language?

Here, Krashen is right. He says, 'we acquire a language, when we understand it'[3] i.e. understand what we read. Perhaps, the learners would like to understand through their own mother tongue what is in English and the English equivalents of mother-tongue. While analysing bilingualism, Krashen says that it is doing well, especially in it (in the two languages), if one is English. In the Indian context it is so. Krashen also says bilingual children do better than all English immersion.[4] This is just to make clear, to the steadfast monolingual English proponents that there is no disadvantage in using the heritage language of a child. A child profits out of it by understanding.

Krashen's usual mantra is 'comprehensible input' and the input has to be very interesting and compelling to read. This kind of reading can be done in the student's L1, as it is more comprehensible than L 2- English. According to Krashen "stories" are the engines that move first and second languages. It is true of learners' first language, whereas, in the second language, it would not go smoothly. For, in the stories of English, there are lots of colloquial conversations and idiomatic expressions, which the ESL students cannot comprehend. Though, teachers use gestures and voice over for some characters, total comprehension like in L1 may not take place. Coming to reading, Krashen emphasizes on self-selected reading, which most of the Indian school students have no access to. For, many schools have no libraries and up to date books. In any case, if the learners are good at first language reading, that would give boost to second language reading also. The language teachers of English are often told that language is need-based, creating a situation, though contrived, to a student is important, so that the student would speak in English.

Let me illustrate an incident. Once a teacher trainer from an advanced learning institute tried to teach some insightful things to teachers. Before her there were students' and teachers sitting in a hall. She called one of the students for a demonstration and said to her (as if to put her in a situation), 'Imagine, you are in Heathrow airport. You have lost your hand bag, money and valuables. You want to make a phone call to your mother; how would you tell your mother over the phone about whatever happened to you in English?' That girl did not answer. Perhaps, she couldn't imagine her being in such a situation. The teacher trainer went on to coax her. 'Don't you feel sad? Don't you want to convey to your mother the pathetic situation you are in' etc. In spite of her prodding for a long time, the girl did not open her mouth. She was just smiling at her because the whole thing was looking farcical to her. Coming from a rural background and also from a poor parentage, she did not know the whereabouts of Heathrow airport and how it looked. Besides, how it would be to lose a purse in an unknown destination and to communicate it in English. In addition, she might not be knowing how to use proper functional items at times of happiness or sadness. It is not only for students, many grown-ups in India are not aware of such nuances of language. Above all, Heathrow airport and London are beyond her reach of understanding, coming from a remote place in Andhra Pradesh. Hence, situations created have to be within students' experiential orbit. In any case, this anecdote was from the pre-internet and social media age in India. In those days, awareness of outside world was very limited.

ELT- Parts to Whole or Whole to Parts?

English in India is taught more as bits and pieces. If students do more and more reading, they get the cohesiveness of the language. Testing language items though situationally would not suffice, to learn the language. For instance, a question like this is asked in their examination for one-mark:

Q) Your friend is leaving for Delhi to take an interview for a job. What would you say to him?

Ans) Put a tick (right mark) against your choice:

a) Congratulations! b) Happy journey! c) Best of luck! d) Don't worry!

These functional aspects have been tested for years. Most of these questions have cut and dried answers. Students invariably learn by rote to get the one mark for this type of question. To them, it is again committing to memory. These are English second language learners. They are learning the mannerisms that are in the English-speaking society. Some of them, of course, are useful in their day-to-day world in Indian context also. But, in the above question, they are all possible answers. Since the friend is going to Delhi, 'happy journey', could also be the answer in some of the students' understanding. The friend may be too nervous to attend the interview, so, 'don't worry', could be the answer to some, as per Indian tradition. In any case, 'best of luck', is the most appropriate and accurate answer, for, we wish a person good luck before a big event. Less likely is, 'congratulations', but feasible, as the friend has come to the level of attending an interview, which the other friend is confident that he would get.

Furthermore, the above functional aspects touched upon during the course of study are not the automatic responses of the student, like how it is done in the student's mother tongue. The greeting or nuances of how to respond to a situation in any language, is language-specific. A bilingual approach would not work in their case. However, it could be explained, as to what expression comes when, in the student's local language. Suppose the student has to say a bigger sentence like: when she meets her friend after a long time, and the friend was successful in getting first in the inter-college badminton competition, how would she have to express her response. Here is the tricky thing. She could say: either, simply, congratulations or 'congratulations on your success in badminton' (in writing). Now, before the word: congratulations, she should get the preposition: "on". These are specific prepositions that go along with specific words in a context. Especially in the case of phrasal verbs, students commit to rote memory that if some woman laughs loudly, they should say, she burst *out* laughing and if the same woman all of a sudden gets tears in her eyes, they should say: she bursts *into* tears etc.

To test functional aspects of grammar, all these types of questions are given in the examination. Since, these kinds of questions recur in the examination question-papers year after year, ESL learners tend to go for rote learning to answer them, as to what appropriate answer comes in which functional situation. In the same way, a schoolchild in a rural area, needs to know through her textbook what to say when, for all greetings. Greetings in English are all frozen/ formulaic expressions. They are taught diligently in 'what would you say' kind of drilling, to greeting someone or for response when, someone greets.

For e.g.

1. If someone says good morning --- Good morning!

2. In a birthday party --- Many happy returns of the day.

3. Your friend is leaving you --- Goodbye!

4. Before going to bed --- Good night!

5. Your friend is suffering from fever --- Wish you a speedy recovery!

6. If someone is getting married --- Congratulations!

7. You attend a marriage (to wish the couple) --- happy married life.

8. Heard an unpleasant news --- Alas!

9. Your team won the match --- Hurrah!

10. Your friend is going on a picnic --- Have a nice day!

Barring good morning/ good afternoon/good night, the others have several ways. These are natural to the children of high English-speaking society. But, for those from other backgrounds, they are to be learnt. Similarly, requests with: Could you please…, would you mind doing…, Suggestions with: It would be better for you…, I would be glad, if you could …, etc., should have to be learnt normally, instead of by rote or learning artificially. These will also be tested in the examinations.

The following question is purely based on grammar. When grammar is not to be taught overtly, this type of pin-pointed questions is tough to answer.

Identify the sentence which has a noun clause.

1.   I went to the hospital to get some medicine.

2.   On his return we asked him some questions.

3.   I went to see what has happened.

4.   I went to see what'd happened. (Correct)

When it comes to pronunciation, stress, intonation etc. an English teacher is the role-model for the students in the class. If that is the case, an English teacher's English should be impeccable. How many teachers are equipped with good English or correct pronunciation or use of language? Private English medium schools will have a select teacher of English, whereas in government schools, only for higher classes, there are exclusively trained teachers for English. These teachers are screened through testing before being taken into service. In the lower classes, students are taught all subjects by one teacher, who may not have the required exposure to the English language. So, the primary school teacher need not necessarily be a model teacher of English.

Kendriya Vidyalayas, run by the central government in India, are schools of good repute. Here, the bilingual method is followed in the initial stages of schooling. At the entry level, these schools take forty percent from regional medium and sixty percent from the English medium. They follow NCERT syllabus i.e. activity-based syllabus. Many teachers take training on "communication and capacity-building in English". Most teachers, nowadays, need training to carry out activities in the English language, or otherwise it is difficult for them. They expect some model lessons by the experts for confidence-building. In special schools like Navodaya schools, as soon as the teachers are selected, they would be sent to Induction Courses.

In the state of Telangana, all state-government-run schools have English as medium from class-1 onwards. Since the government knows about the disability of students in English, the Telangana State School Education Department is providing bilingual textbooks i.e. textbooks in two languages: Telugu and English for all non-language subjects like mathematics, science and social studies. The two versions are made available for easier understanding. For example, each page of a lesson in Telugu medium will have an English version on the adjacent page as well. These bilingual textbooks, according to officials, will help non-English medium students transition to English medium, besides helping them better understand and learn topics with ease.[5]

In support of bilingualism, academicians say …bilingualism per se involves no cognitive penalties and that it is a capacity that can be almost effortlessly acquired by the young children. Bilingualism is a rational and practical response to diversity. Hence, in the initial stages a child's mother tongue is essential, for, it is in the child's everyday conversational language. Of late, in India, 'the University Grants Commission (UGC) has asked universities to allow students to write exams in local/regional languages even if the course is offered in English medium, while arranging evaluators and encouraging the translation of textbooks,'…[6] So, therefore, the need for bilingualism is more pronounced, as a policy measure at present.

---

1. N. Krishnaswamy, An Introduction to Linguistics For Language Teachers - Teaching A Second Language: Methodology, SOMAIYA PUBLICATIONS PVT LTD, Bombay, 1971, reprinted 1980, pp 215-216.

2. https://slideplayer.com/slide/7505157/

3. https://www.youtube.com/watch?v=9XR_fb1fv1g

4.   https://www.youtube.com/watch?v=9XR_fb1fv1g

5.   https://telanganatoday.com/textbooks-in-telangana-govt-schools-to-go-bilingual

6.   https://www.hindustantimes.com/education/news/allow-exams-to-be-written-in-local-languages-for-english-medium-courses-too-ugc-101681908769046-amp.html

Chapter-12

Multilingualism in ELT

Multilingualism (Multilingual Language Education - MLE) is now emphasized more in the New Education Policy (NEP 2020) in India than earlier, although it was recognised as compatible within the Indian framework of school curriculum. India as a land of multiple languages, its very identity is linguistic diversity. Linguistic diversity in India is a unifying factor. The unifying thread is the culture. The same cultural values are expressed in different languages. That is the reason the Sahitya Akademi, that was set-up soon after Independence, as the central nodal agency for all Indian-language-literatures, contains the motto: *"Indian literature is one, written in many languages."* That shows the innate unity in all Indian languages.

In India, multiple languages complement each other in meeting the communicative needs of the people, says Dr Ajit K Mohanty of Jawaharlal Nehru University (JNU). He writes, in his book "The Multilingual Reality: Living with Languages" that, 'Multilingualism and language-in-education policies and practices in the subcontinent are affected by a hierarchical relationship of languages characterized by a double divide – one between English and the major national/regional languages and the other between the major languages and the indigenous tribal minority (ITM) ones.'[1]

For the above predicament, Prof Sarah G. Thomson, linguist, University of Michigan says, 'Among countries where many languages are spoken, endangerment of some or most of the minority languages is probable'. She also adds reclaiming threatened languages is possible. In any case, the language –speaking community should have the will to revive and reclaim.[2] All in all, languages are expressions of norms, conditions and traditions. That is their underlying essence. The identity of India i.e. Bharat is a civilization. The culture is based on civilization. In India's tradition different uses of languages are welcome. Elsewhere in the world, multilingual speech communities differ from each other in so many ways. No language is singular in nature. It is manifested as per the situation. Sanskrit and Hindi are synonymous.

For many Indian languages, Sanskrit is the source language. Indians are by birth multilinguals. For, when a Bengali lives in Andhra, he talks Bengali at home, Telugu in the market, Hindi if he meets a North Indian and English too in the office for all official purposes. Hence, as the linguist J.A. Fishman said: *who speaks what language to whom and when in a multilingual society is note-worthy.* As a matter of fact, India is a garden of languages. Of course, occasionally, some parochial, chauvinistic passions are whipped up by the vested interest, for narrow political gains. Indians should also be mindful of conflicts arising out of such linguistic chauvinism. Some linguists opine that language is Janus-faced. For, language is culturally a means of enrichment, politically, it could be a very emotive issue that generates identity conflicts. However, these mind-boggling languages in India and their independent identities have never been a problem for the country's unity and integrity. Indeed, they were never a cause for concern, as the thread underlying them is almost the same social and cultural life. India's unity is not something forced upon it from outside, to being 'one' nation. It is its innate civilizational strength coming through thousands of years. India after Independence, has consciously and conscientiously tried to nurture its languages for preserving the rich culture of the country. The three-language formula was introduced in the Constitution. Notwithstanding, there was opposition to the formula from many states. Tamil Nadu resisted Hindi language in school curriculum and perceived it as an imposition from the North. Similarly, North-Indian states were reluctant to learn southern languages.

The first Prime Minister, Pandit Jawaharlal Nehru was against the formation of linguistic states i.e. states-formed on the basis of language. Earlier, during colonial rule India had provincial states, where there was an amalgamation of two three Indian languages. The Madras presidency consisted of Tamil, Telugu, and Kannada. The Bombay presidency had Marathi, Telugu Gujarati etc. The fear for demarcating linguistic states was that it could lead to the narrow parochial and chauvinistic feelings among people within such a state. So, therefore, it would not help in promoting the much-desired holistic national goals and aspirations.

Hence, after independence, the first prime minister wanted intermingling. Yet, people would tend to identify more with language than with the region. Late Mr. C.P Bhambhri, noted columnist, in his article: "Withering of language-based states"- 2010 supported the initial language –based policy (for the formation of linguistic states) that was fought for. He writes, 'It deserves to be clearly understood that human beings emotionally identify themselves with their own language and literature, and language–based identity can be a viable basis for democratic governance of a country or a region within a country.'[3]

When Telugu and Tamil speaking regions together were in the Madras Presidency, Telugu-speaking people felt they were discriminated against, in the predominantly Tamil-speaking Madras state. For having a separate state for Telugu speaking people i.e. Visala Andhra statehood was sought and fought for. Late Shri. Potti Sriramulu was known for sacrificing his life by fasting unto death to attain the desired objective of attaining the Telugu-state. At the beginning of Sriramulu's steadfast *satyagraha*, Nehru did not relent. Finally, when Sriramulu succumbed to his life, there was a huge surge of anger among Telugu people that was displayed on the streets. Nehru, then under pressure, agreed to the statehood for the Telugu-speaking in 1956. Thus, linguistic states came into existence. That was the beginning of linguistic states in India. Linguistic states are primarily to sustain and promote the state language, culture and state-specific traditions together, as one unique community. Every language community has its rich culture and tradition to take pride in and nurture. It gives a sense of belongingness. The rich literature of each language and the pearls of wisdom that comes out from it, is a treasure to preserve. The contributions of artists and artisans, poets, musicians and dancers, paintings and sculpture are their legacy and property to keep up.

As a consequence of linguistic states, people have become content with their own language. Therefore, they have become monolingual. Otherwise, each provincial state under the British had two or three Indian languages overlapped. The Nizam state had Kannada, Maharashtrian and Telangana regions in it. Similarly, Andhra had a border with parts of Odia in the north and two, three districts: Gulbarga, Bidar etc. of present-day Karnataka. Even now, in Chittoor district of Andhra Pradesh, which borders Tamil Nadu, people speak both Tamil and Telugu with the same ease. Code-switching from one language to the other takes place without a conscious effort. Most often, code-switching and code-mixing---these two happen in bilinguals and multilinguals. One language has an impact on the other. Because, language and society are inseparable. 'For, code- switching and code-mixing you must have two or more languages. Code-switching is to switch from one utterance in one language to another in another language. Whereas, code-mixing is overlapping of a word of one language with the other. For e.g.: start in Hindi get a word which belongs to the overlapping area. Switch words inconsequentially. For instance: posemarafy – pose is an English word, marafy is a Hindi word'.[4]

The western countries are all monolingual. According to them, multilingual societies are less harmonious than the monolingual ones. In the 19th century, the myth developed that a nation-state is monolingual not by its creation but 'by mere nature', and that monolingualism in the national language is the 'natural' result of being born and growing up in a nation-state. 'In the U.S., enthusiasm for multilingualism is entirely different. It is partly a liberal reaction to the country's steadfast monolingual culture. There are many ethnic groups in the U.S., whose first language is not English. Yet, they sought to learn English and assimilate.[5]

In the West, a nation-state should have only one language. And that language is the national and official language of that particular country. As in France-French, Germany-German, Spain-Spanish ... so on. The national language is invariably the spoken language of the people. This national language policy is mandatory. In that language, their leaders and people speak. The very purpose of having this one-state-language (monolingual) is, what the leaders in those countries speak, the people understand and what the people speak leaders understand. Along with, for communication of any programme or policy-measures, especially their political leaders, do not struggle hard. Unlike in India, they do not need any translators. In translation some of what the original speaker said is lost. In spite of all, the disadvantage of having monolingualism is the loss of multilingualism in those countries. Those countries also have several languages. But they preferred one dominant language suppressing others.

In India language boundaries are porous. Language is fluid. There is nothing called monolingualism in the Indian context. Multilingualism is common. It is not a collection of languages, but it is a concept of mind, says a noted linguist.

He adds, languages flourish in each other's company. To an extent every person in India is multilingual. India is a rich country with a rich linguistic landscape. In India, there are four language families: Indo-Aryan, Dravidian, Tibeto- Burman, Tai-Kadai. There is no other place in the world where there are so many language families and still are porous as one. In language learning the objective should be, whether the child is able to say something. That is necessary, according to multilingualism.

Independent-India aspired Hindi to be the national language

Following the western modal, Indian post-independent leaders wished to have Hindi as the Indian national language. Hindi, being widely spoken in North-India, the language rightly gets national identity. But there was stiff opposition from southern states, especially from Tamil Nadu. As a result, Hindi has become the national official language, along with associate official language English, which the southern states could understand. During those days of independence, all the national leaders including Gandhi ji, though being a Gujarati and having written many of his books and literature in Gujarati and English, wanted Hindi to be the national language. The dithering of Pandit Jawaharlal Nehru by listening to both parties from the North and South of India, could not make much of a headway in declaring Hindi as national language. This hesitation is captured by KR Srinivasa Iyengar. He writes, 'This marvellous capacity (of Nehru) to see both sides of every question was a priceless blessing indeed, though it often weakened Jawaharlal's power of action…The language question was a case … (Nehru stated) None of the regional languages---not even Hindi---should be newly put in a position of superiority over the others'.[6] Further Srinivas Iyengar wrote, Since, however, we need an 'official language' for inter-state purposes, it might as well continue to be English, since it … has many other advantages as well'.[7] From then onwards, English continued as an official language. Later Hindi became the official language and English the associate language. Even today, in High Courts and Supreme Court of India, the proceedings take place and judgements are delivered in English.

In a way, the South Indians resisted Hindi to be the official language for the whole of India, because that may lead them to read Hindi compulsorily for the top examinations like: The Union Public Service Commission (UPSC) to become civil servants and also for other Central Government posts. They would have to compete in Hindi-writing and speaking with the mother tongue Hindi language speakers. That seemed to have been a huge task. Undoubtedly, mother tongue speakers would have an edge over others. However, the above fears seemed to be unfounded. For every theory there is an available counter-theory. At present, in the state of Telangana, the government (after the formation of the state) established Muslim minority English medium residential schools, where Urdu is the first language. As per the reservation policy applied to SC & ST students, Telugu speaking SC & ST students can get admitted in them (of course, initially without the knowledge of Urdu being the first language in those schools many joined). Nonetheless, most of the Telugu mother tongue students, it is said, are scoring better marks in Urdu than the Muslim students, whose mother tongue is Urdu. Similarly, in the Telugu medium schools Muslims fare better in Telugu subject than some of the Telugu speaking. Here, the aptitude of the student is important. Most of the time, one would learn the other Indian language, better than their own in schools. For, they learn systematically, methodically and formally by the syntax and grammar than the mother-tongue speakers. Hence, students tend to learn languages other than their own mother tongue with precision. This is about learning how to write. While speaking, mother tongue speakers have an advantage, as they learn naturally at home.

In any case, to replace English with Hindi totally in India is difficult, as science and technology need the support of English. Spoken Hindi is most prevalent in India and elsewhere with the Non-Resident Indians (NRIs) in other parts of the world. This is partly because movies, media and T.V. channels dish out many interesting soap operas in Hindi, which non-Hindi speaking people also would like to watch with keen intent. The performance of the actors at national level and story value also makes people interested to see irrespective of language. Unconsciously, language acquisition takes place. The thinking in the past was: eventually, 'Hindi will grow in good time, and perhaps one day by virtue of its richness and strength become the de facto lingua franca of India.'[8] Of course, India is moving in that direction slowly.

After The Introduction of English-Education in India

Indian languages have a rich culture and heritage which is unique to this country. After the introduction of Macaulay's famous 1835 education minutes, the scenario in education changed to a great extent. His introduction of English education and his derision for Indian education has definitely changed the landscape. Though English education started off with limited convents, it has later spread to other private educational institutions. The private players came in and competed with the government educational institutions i.e. government-run schools and won the battle. The private-English medium schools sprouted all over.

After the Liberalization in the 1990s, people started getting information from across the skies through internet satellite cable T.V. channels. Awareness among the people has grown tremendously. Once upon a time, English was only limited to the elite of India. The prominence of the market-driven English language has grown. The middle classes became affluent because of the upward mobility, post-liberalisation. As a consequence, English has been percolated to the middle classes. English from the beginning has been the *lingua franca* in India, but its importance grew far more. 'English (now) is seen as an access route to the middle classes and geographical mobility within India and beyond,'[9] writes David Graddol.

India, apart from its many other hierarchical differences, this new schism of English speaking and non-English speaking has widened. The poor and downtrodden began thinking English language to be an enabler and a vehicle for upward mobility. To them, it is a panacea for all the ills around them. This trend for English Medium, A.K. Mohanty says, is perpetuating a new caste system. There is a double-divide between English and vernacular: English is pushing other major languages in the country and other major languages are pushing tribal languages to the corner without any of their growth. The Dalits built a temple for the goddess of English to worship. All in all, English has become a language of aspiration. When all pervading -English is looming large, many right-thinking people are worried about what would happen to native Indian languages. Would they survive the onslaught of English or would they fade away--- is the dilemma? These concerns were expressed in many forums. Some views regarding the revival of Indian languages are as the following:

1. The government of India should formulate the 'Language Education Policy'. In each state, if non-natives speak the natives' language, they should be appreciated and honoured.

2. India is a *darshan* (panoramic view) of all languages and traditions, the country is known for its tolerance and universal acceptance, 'Bharat is a *Darshan*'- in reality.

3. There is a lot of debate going on in the country, on how a market-oriented language (English) is side-lining the mother tongue. By mechanically following the western-model, Indians are not critically thinking of what is happening.

4. When Indian languages are going to be eliminated by the dominance and onslaught of the English language, it is extremely problematic. In India we have no single language to speak throughout the country. Hence, a comprehensive policy is needed.

5. Peoples' languages or mother tongues are seriously neglected. They are going to be endangered, since India has no language policy in the country. Hence, multilingualism should be promoted. It creates the child with more intelligence and more cognitive effects. Even researchers say to that effect.

6. Hindi and Urdu are not different; they only have two different scripts. At the ground level, they are the same. Arabic has nothing in common with Urdu more than it has with Persian.

7. In India only scheduled languages get patronage from the government whereas non-scheduled languages do not. So, tribals opt for bilingualism leading to language loss of one of their languages.

8. Interestingly, studies show that Indians get dementia at a late age, compared to Americans. Because multilingualism works on their cognitive domain better.

9. Mother tongue works on ecosystems also. If a student is asked to name ten birds in English, he takes time, whereas, in mother-tongue, he says

quickly with ease. That shows that for conservation of environment, flora and fauna, mother-tongue is important.

10. Mahatma Gandhi's words on English education are often quoted. According to Gandhiji, 'the English-education-mask has emasculated the English-educated Indian, putting a strain on his nerves and energy. With imitators (of English), no country can rise. The whole nation is emasculated. We can never become a proper Bharat'.

The above fears are also prevalent in Africa and in the entire continent of Europe. The European Union has twenty-seven member countries with twenty-three official and eighty other European languages, other than the UK (now with Brexit, it is no more in EU), they are all observing the same plight. David Graddol in his book: *English Next India*, compares India's complexity and language policy problem with that of Europe. He writes, There is a growing parallel between India and Europe in terms of language policy ... and the rising demand for English... the curriculum in European countries is now dominated by the need to learn English,'[10] So, therefore in Europe they are encouraging bilingual schools. Earlier French had enjoyed the status of official language for the European Union; now it has been taken over by the English, causing the English divide in the EU countries, as is clear from his writing. Graddol further adds, One of the biggest challenges in language policy in Europe is now how to balance the universal need for English with the equal need to maintain the vitality of each of the other languages... The European Union is in principle committed to strengthening multilingualism at all levels of European education systems, ...'[11]

A small excerpt on Indian languages

The British-India had done the first comprehensive survey of languages in India and published 19 volumes from 1898 to 1928. It was headed by George Abraham Grierson. The survey stated that there were 364 languages and dialects. After independence, the Constitution of India in its list of Schedule-VIII has 22 languages. Linguistic states were created in India in 1956 but today there are 29 states for 22 languages. Gradually, since independence there has been a depletion of languages and dialects, as they are not given due importance or patronage. Minor languages in a state are gobbled by hegemonic regional languages.

The overarching influence of English is not encouraging for the regional languages to fully blossom. After independence, the 1961 Census Report listed a total of 1652 mother tongues in India. Whereas, after ten years, the 1971 Census listed only 108 languages. The more recent one is the People's Linguistic Survey of India, started in the year 2010, and has identified 780 languages and 86 scripts in India. Hence, there is an imminent need and urgency to protect the languages in India. Multilingualism as a policy measure in education helps to take this forward.[12]

In Continuous Professional Development Programs (CPDs) teachers are made aware of the uses of multilingualism like: multilingualism is an aid in the English classroom and not a hindrance. Multilingualism promotes: scholastic achievement, cognitive growth and societal tolerance. In fact, languages flourish in one another's company and die if they are frozen in textbooks, dictionaries and grammar books. In a multilingual class, teachers should make use of strategies like: translation, paraphrase, code-mixing, code-switching, very effectively. Teachers need to consider multilingualism as a great source for him or her in teaching the target language. Teachers also need to amalgamate the multiplicity of languages, cultural practices and ethos. They could use it as a great resource to foster: social tolerance, linguistic enhancement, cooperative and collaborative reading. Every child speaking a different language can voice it and feel that he or she is given proper space in the classroom.

Dispelling the false assumptions:

1. English can be taught only through the medium of English … is a false notion. In fact, to acquire a language, there is no need for more input but comprehensible input is necessary.

2. It is not easy to teach English in a multilingual context … is wrong. For, English teachers need to be: patient, resourceful, innovative.

3. Pupils belonging to tribal areas and backward areas cannot acquire English easily … is a misconception. It is totally based on preconceived notions and a prejudiced opinion. Anybody can learn any language depending on his or her: need and motivation to learn the language.

Multilingual classrooms--- student participation--- and other factors:

Multilingualism in the classroom is good, in the sense, that it gives an opportunity to every child to speak. The academician view is that, 'every child speaking a different language can voice it and feel that she or he is given proper space in the classroom'. This is what should happen in a classroom. Speaking to teachers happens with children from elite backgrounds in elite schools. It happens so, for, they are groomed or being given the choice to air their views on different subjects by their educated parents. To discuss and debate over contemporary issues is a matter of privilege. Children that come to government schools though they possess some views in whatever way i.e., haphazardly, they are brought up in a society that gives no room to air. Not only the poor, even the middle-class in India, are brought up in a culture, where freedom of speech is construed as being emboldened or impolite. It is not that they do not have at all. But it is within the bounds.

Usually in classrooms, whatever the teacher teaches, students take it unquestioningly, in the ordinary Indian school-context. Here, culture plays the role. Not only in India but also in many countries of Asia this culture is all pervading. In a paper on *Attitudes toward Question Answering and Classroom Interaction in the English Classroom...*' a professor in K K University writes, students like, directed learning, more than, discussed learning, (according to learners) teachers should teach because they have higher experience than students, … '[13] If this is the opinion based on the university students of English, one could well imagine for a schoolchild. Assume, even if multilingual approach is followed, participating in a discussion and airing an opinion on the subject is not an easy task.

Here (in this paper), he mentioned the various research studies conducted in English classroom interactions in Honkong, Thailand and other Asian countries. Students rarely participate to ask questions and nobody volunteers to answer questions. He also draws a conclusion which says, the crucial point related to Asian culture is different from the Western culture. In Asian culture children have to obey and respect adults and showing silence means acceptance. The maxim of modesty is one issue for interaction of Asian people and that is the problem to communicate and participate in the English classrooms.' While partly agreeing with what he said, there is also a culture in ancient India that seeks knowledge through questions. To cite the Hindu Upanishads, they are dialogic i.e. by way of question answers. In any open-society, questioning is allowed. Indeed, in this sub-continent the questioning should not appear to be rude or impolite. Whether this discipline is for good or bad, is debatable.

To make students talk in the class, the teacher should create teaching - learning in a relaxed atmosphere i.e. the atmosphere should be non-threatening to the learners. Teachers should be precise and be clear with questions. They should be easy to comprehend and interesting to answer. The teacher should encourage activities like: role playing, presentations, discussions (in higher classes), cooperative/ group- learning and other techniques. More than anything, the teacher's behaviour should be friendly and courteous. This makes the students confident to ask questions or to answer what the teacher asks them to. Furthermore, the teacher's attitude counts in students' participation. The teacher's questions in higher classes should be such that they help students to develop their language ability both inside and outside the classroom. Students should be encouraged to learn on their own by using self- learning methods of listening to news or watching television (an audio-visual), learning from the internet or items of importance in social media to enhance their English language capability. Certainly, multilingual teaching will help and enable the said activities. Moreover, Professor Marian, one of the pioneers in the field of psycholinguistics and has been studying multilingual brains since the 1990s, she in her book "The Power of Language: Multilingualism, Self and Society" writes, according to her research, the multilingual brain functions very differently from the "standard" monolingual brain when it comes to memory, decision-making, creativity, aging and more.[14]

1.   https://www.researchgate.net/publication/319389354_Language_Policy_and_Education_in_the_Indian_Subcontinent

2.   https://www.youtube.com/live/F_LxZmtRXZk?si=Bg8MDrLJEoVJi_Uh

3.   *https://m.economictimes.com/opinion/et-commentary/withering-of-language-based-states/articleshow/54505*

4. INDIAN MULTILINGUALISM: ACQUISITION AND IMPLICATIONS
    S.N. Sridhar Stony Brook University s.sridhar@stonybrook.edu p.14,

5. https://www.tandfonline.com/doi/full/10.1080/07908318.2021.
    1979578?src=recsys

6. KR Srinivasa Iyengar 1995, Introduction p.13, Indian Writing in English,
    Sterling Publishers Pvt. Ltd., New Delhi-110016, p. 307

7. Ibid p. 307

8. Ibid p.14

9. English Next India, David Graddol. p.14

10. Ibid p. 58

11. Ibid p.59

12. https://www.education.gov.in/en/sites/upload_files/mhrd/files/upload_
    document/languagebr.pdf

13. Attitudes toward Question Answering and Classroom Interaction in the
    English Classroom of Thai University Students Chalong Rattanapong
    1(songsak_rattanapong@hotmail.com) Thapakorn The Suriwong 2
    (tipakornt@yahoo.com)

14. https://www.euronews.com/culture/2023/04/05/the-power-of-language-5-
    ways-multilingual-brains-work-differently

Chapter-13

The Necessity of Multilingualism in the Present Scenario

(Endangerment to world and Indian Languages - Danger is Looming Large)

For a long time, the teaching of ESL in India has been only in English, although L1 has been used unofficially by some teachers. These 'English alone' classes have been, only, to promote the target language English for ESL learners. Now, English is emerging gigantic all over the world and in India, making the native languages trifling. Hence, the trend of teaching English has been changing, in accordance, with the time into the multilingual culture. In multilingual countries, the course correction is: to encourage the indigenous languages along with English. This way, students feel at home to use their own language without shyness or inhibition to express themselves in the class. Right now, 'The world is divided into two linguistic blocks, the Dominant Monolingual and the Multilingual. They operate under two logics: Either-Or and Both-And. One results in hierarchical relations, the other in complementary relations. Multilingualism can be sustained only if languages are in complementary relation.'[1]

Multilingualism through decades of educational policies

'Celebrating multilingualism is not enough, Indians should also be mindful of endangered languages in the country declared by the United Nations. India heads the list of countries in the Atlas of the world's languages in danger (UNESCO 2009). Loss of languages is considered by many as a "natural" outcome of organic decay of languages', writes A.K. Mohanty.[2]

National Curriculum Framework (NCF) 2005 also lays its emphasis on the promotion of multilingualism. NCF 2005 says, 'Multilingualism, which is constitutive of the identity of a child and a typical feature of the Indian linguistic landscape… the best use of a resource readily available…'[3] It further states, 'Several studies have shown that bilingual proficiency raises the levels of cognitive growth, social tolerance, divergent thinking and scholastic achievement.'[4] NCF 2023 (nearly two-decades after NCF 2005) reiterates what NEP 2020 states, on multi-lingual teaching classrooms. The National Education Policy (NEP) 2020 explicitly guides language development in schools to focus on teaching many languages and developing multilingual capacities. It says, 'As … multilingualism has great cognitive benefits to young students, children will be exposed to different languages early on (but with a particular emphasis on the mother tongue), starting from the Foundational Stage onwards…'[5]

English in day-to-day life

The prevailing atmosphere in the country is conducive to multilingualism, as with the upward mobility, people are doing business in many parts of the country. For them, though they hire locals, it becomes imperative to learn the language of that particular region, to conduct their business effectively. As Joshua Fishman put it, 'if you want to buy, you can do it in any language but if you want to sell, know your customer language.'[6] The other reason for acquisition of a language is the media. Hindi is the predominant language in India and also the official language of the country. Hindi films have been seen and appreciated in many countries and from across all states of India. The viewership is huge. Moreover, subconsciously the Hindi language acquisition takes place through watching them. Hindi is gaining momentum throughout India, like never before because of Hindi movies and T.V. shows. To many people in India, using two or three languages at a time by code-switching and code-mixing has become a common thing. Most often, Hindi and English are used interchangeably on national English television channels. Many in India acquire a working knowledge of English, because it is taught in all schools, as a second language. So far as to express themselves; they could freely do so in their mother tongue. In fact, English is not culturally akin to India. Many well-versed pundits in English, though they see news bulletins in English and read English newspapers, when it comes to entertainment, they switch over to local Indian languages i.e. either mother tongue or Hindi or any other Indian language. They wouldn't mind their little knowledge in the other

Indian language-channels (other than that of their mother-tongue) on which they see a movie or soap-opera or some kind of jovial clipping. Why? Because they can relate their Indian environs (villages, roads, buses, milk booths, houses, cots, beds, men and women by their attire etc.) Therefore, the local languages that get the picture of the locale of the Indian society, give an edge over English. On the other hand, English language specific idiomatic language-use is difficult to understand. It is an uphill task for average Indians. Unless one immerses oneself in the language, the idioms will not become natural to them. Such immersion and native-like English acquisition could only take place for Indians in English-speaking countries or the most elite English-speaking class or for those Indians that go frequently on business trips to those lands.

Most Indians feel free in their own mother tongue. Often the so-called English Professors, who speak with flawless pronunciation (as per phonology) before students, at home they tend to shed that sophistication, while using English terms. That is to say, to offer a correct skill or way of pronouncing, the teacher makes a conscious effort on her part. While at home in her natural self, with no conscious effort, the way she uses the words is different. Because in their mother tongue, their accent changes, as per the nuances of their mother tongue/ first language (L1). English-humour is subtle to understand for an average Indian. English movies, though worth watching for English language enthusiasts, for the English language value, but not many could understand. Many Indians would not prefer them for entertainment. Native language channels are preferred, as they are easier to grasp and do not tax their brain. Native language channels also touch the chord. English humour, as many people say, is fine. But only the English can appreciate it. Of course, there are some Indians who adopted English almost or more than their mother tongue in India, and may understand to a greater extent. Here, Indians who settled abroad in English-speaking countries are excluded. For, they could understand English as well as Indian wit and humour. They are used to the English language surroundings in their adopted country. Since they had spent their early childhood in India, they carry the language and culture to the lands they have chosen to settle. As a matter of fact, they are the carriers of old Indian culture at a distance.

To say how difficult it is for local Indians to acquire English, there is an interesting anecdote from the British era. When the English ruled India, they were the bosses', somewhat educated - Indians were their subordinates to help them and to make bridges with the ordinary masses. The English laid the railways for India. One day, an English officer on a trip, got down at a Railway station. He was irritated by the litter around on the platform making it dirty and filthy. Getting angry, he shouted at the top of his voice:

'Who is the station-master here? Who is the station-master here?'

The stationmaster, an Indian, came running and said, 'I is the station-master here'.

Then, the English officer said, 'Oh! You are the station-master here'.

Then the station-master corrected himself and said, 'I are the station-master here'.

Perhaps, the station-master was in a hurry to answer the angry officer, perhaps, he was worried, what would the officer do to him or to his job; perhaps he was not aware of the English language grammar much, he committed two-mistakes in his answers, given twice. These mistakes, one would not make in his mother tongue, however much, a person is in tension.

Three-Language formula in Indian education

Though the three-language formula, as an education policy is followed in most of the southern states, a large section of the population, who have not gone formally to schools i.e. older people of yester generation, remained monolingual. This is seen mainly in rural areas. This poses a problem. For, the central government employees, on transfer, move around to different parts of the country. They come from different language backgrounds. They sometimes need to interact with people. They cannot interact with the locals in rural areas because of language-barrier. Suppose, a central government employee of Tamil/ Hindi/ Marathi-speaking, is posted in a Telugu-speaking state, if he had to conduct a survey door to door on behalf of the government, how would he manage the local language? Or if he would like to know the inherent problems of any scheme meant for them, how would he assess? He needs to take a translator. In his own country, he needed someone else's help. A question arises here: is the encouragement of multilingualism in school education the answer? Yes, to an extent. Is the encouragement to promote English to all, so that the educated next generation have no problem at all, as English becomes a link language for all? No. There are inherent difficulties in learning English. To get the kind of fluency and expression in English, like that of mother tongue and to convey one's own thoughts, is difficult for many sections of Indians. Had English been easy, all Indians would have learnt it by now i.e. after two-hundred long years of British rule.

There are other ways and means to promote multilingualism, if seriously intended. Way back, the Dakshin Bharat Hindi Prachar Sabha, vigorously promoted Hindi language in erstwhile united Andhra Pradesh and awarded certificates after passing the Prathama, Madhyamika, Rashtra Basha and Pravesa to name a few of its courses. Many Telugu speaking people willingly learnt Hindi. One, for want of learning the national language (Hindi) that comes handy, when they visit North Indian states. Sometimes, when they go on pilgrimages or for touring historically important sites, Hindi language is helpful. The other reason being: getting a certificate. Indians always consider certificates as important add-ons to their resume'. Likewise, the state-governments could promote their own languages, in other states, that are contiguous. They may fix a cash award with each certificate to incentivise learners. This way, many would learn in the evening or whenever it is convenient to them, by going to the centres, where they are established or from apps that promote the language and write the examination for certification. Thus, by knowing the language, they could work in other states of India.

Years ago, Late Chief Minister of Andhra Pradesh (united), N.T. Rama Rao, wanted to promote Telugu, the state-language. So, he passed an official order stating that whoever studies in the Telugu medium of instruction (some of them used to take their graduation degree also in Telugu) would be added, additional five marks in the service commission examinations, while recruiting for employment in the state services. The youth were, then, jubilant of the decision taken. For, they had studied in their mother- tongue/regional medium, as it was the only medium available, through which, education was imparted in rural areas. To compete with the urban English-educated and to write English examination-paper along with them, in the competitive service-commission-examinations, was no ordinary task. That kind of decision would help for the promotion of the mother tongue/regional languages. However, that was all past history of the1980s. That was the pre-Liberalisation and pre-Globalisation era. Now, with awareness, and in the impression that English language enables them to get a decent job and status in the society, many are opting for it. At present, the exodus from the regional-mediums to the English medium is no-holds-barred.

However, study after study shows mother-tongue education is better than education in English medium. 'An eight-year study on Latin American-origin students in the United States found that there was an "inverse relation between exposure to English instruction and English achievement". This meant students who were taught in primary school using Spanish actually did better at English than Latin American-origin students who were taught in English from the beginning.'[7] To contain these large sections of masses and to convince them that it is through their mother tongue a child could understand the complicated theories and concepts of science and mathematics, is a huge task. The Pratham survey report on class-v students, not able to read class-ii books fluently or do double digit multiplications, is all to be blamed on the way education is imparted. To this day, in villages where the survey's findings come from, the learning in primary schools is in learners' mother tongue/regional language. Then, where is the lacuna? It's not the medium alone; it is the way education is imparted that's questionable. That's the reason for concentrating on "quality in education". Let there be incentives. Those who studied up to v or viii, in the mother tongue/regional medium, are given admission in the universities with an advantage of five to ten points/marks extra or so suitably during their selection. After all, it is said that in the U.S., some kind of preferential treatment is given to the candidates, whose basic education is in their public schools. Hence, multilingualism as a promotional policy of the government, is in the hands of the government. It's really a good idea to push through. Otherwise, with these new English schools emerging in India, India would get a new creole of English. Or otherwise the rural population would eventually be speaking some pidgin-type of English.

Pidgins and Creoles

Here, it is better to understand how pidgins and creoles are formed. Because of colonization, Europeans have come into contact with the natives, in the countries they ruled. Pidgin and creole languages arose, in situations, where the native language came into contact with English (or Spanish, French etc.). Pidgin is a simplified link language, not fully developed. When a pidgin becomes a mother tongue, it is a creole. Pidgin is a language between the rulers and the ruled or between traders.

The etymology of pidgins---how the word originated:[8], The Chinese could not pronounce 'business'/bizniz/, they would say instead 'pidgin' /pidzin/.[9] Chinese mispronunciation of the word led to pidgin. In pidgins, reduction and simplification of language happens. Those that speak pidgin language do:

1. Omission of grammatical words, but retain lexical words.

2. Omit for nouns, the plural morphemes.

3. No possessive marker.

4. No concordial markers,

5. Don't distinguish between: me /I/ my.

6. double-negatives etc.

7. One dominant superior and inferior is mixed: link language hierarchy.

8. Pidgin type of simplified English is spoken by: butlers in hotels, domestic servants in elite families, tourist guides, taxi-drivers in Metros.

A pidgin language is, by definition, one whose structure and lexicon (words) have been drastically reduced, and which is native to none of those who use it. (For e.g.: butler English in India).

A creole, likewise by definition, is a pidgin language which has become the native language of a specific community. Both pidgins and creoles have clearly definable and describable grammatical structures, which, however, differ markedly from those of the 'full-sized' source-languages from which they are historically derived.[10]

Sanskrit is the source-language to many of the Indian languages. But none of the Indian languages are either pidgins or creoles of Sanskrit. Most are independent languages, though drawing some of their lexicon and structure from Sanskrit. Precisely, that was the reason all Indian languages are connected. So are Indians.

All said and done, English is the second language in India. There is a well-known saying about second language learning: 'Learning a second Language is like marrying a second time'.[11] The mind of the second language learner is not a clean slate. Already principles that are underlying in the first language are in his mind, is the common perception of many linguists. Certainly, studying English, as a second language, is different in India. Even for a high school learner there is not much transfer of skills from L1 to L2 i.e. English. Some academicians assume that bilingualism helps the socially backward sections of India to learn English. But that does not seem to be the case either. As per Cummins interdependence principles of language learning, if analysed ... 'Transfer of linguistic and cognitive skills is facilitated in bilingual programs. Once students have basic literacy skills in the L1 and communicative skills in the L2, they can begin reading and writing in the L2, efficiently transferring the literacy skills they have acquired in the familiar language.'[12]

Here, the vital points to be noted are:

1. 'Basic literacy skills in the L1

    And

2. Communicative skills in the L2'.

In India, many high school students have, neither 'communicative skills in the L2 i.e., English' nor 'oral L2- English skills are developed'. Then how can the efficient transfer of linguistic and cognitive skills of L1 facilitate L2 learning?

Grammar skill transfer from L 1 to L2

Most academic scholars' views on grammar are:

'Grammar is substantially the same in all languages, even though it may vary accidentally; whoever knows grammar in one language knows it in another so far as its substance is concerned'.[13]

If a student cannot speak in the second language (L2), it is because of the words and their formations. However, by learning English grammar alone, a student cannot speak. She has to plunge into the language like how a swimmer dives into the pool to swim. Can the swimmer dive into the pool, merely learning by rote the rules of how to swim from a book? No. She has to negotiate the way forward in the pool slowly, by using the appropriate strokes learnt from the rule-book. First, easier ones. Later, after learning and experiencing practically, the difficult ones. That is, one of the principles in education: simple to complex. Swimming is a skill. Language learning is also skill-based. Learning in one's mother tongue is easier because it is more direct. As Jespersen stated, language acquisition takes place right from childhood. That language acquisition leads to language learning. Once the established first language is in the student's mind and that is used for all purposes, she doesn't feel the need or pinch to learn the second language. English as a second language is learnt mainly because it is in the curriculum and it will improve the final score of pass percentage. Of course, there are other students, who may have the aptitude to learn English for better prospects in life. For some it may be a fad to speak in it.

Different multilingual contexts--- India vis-à-vis the West

Most of the western-writers that write on multilingualism, write from the point of view of English-speaking countries. For them, the migrants are from different countries. The children of these immigrants hold on to their mother tongue, spoken by their parents at home. In the U.S., the immigrants from Mexico speak Spanish. On the other hand, English is the national language in the U.S. Since the U.S. is a monolingual country, schoolchildren have no choice but to study in English. That's their difficulty. If these children are taught in their respective mother-tongues, along with English., that's multilingualism. Juxtapose this to the Indian scenario. In India, Indian languages dominate in speaking and writing. In most of the schools, English is taught as a subject, but it has no environment around, like in that of the western countries. In this scenario, if the class becomes bilingual or multilingual, the role of English is reduced. Many teachers in government-run schools teach English in the students' mother-tongue i.e. the local language. Hence, multilingualism in India, is different from the multilingualism of the West.

For immigrant children in the U.S. learning English is a question of survival, for an Indian student it is not so. Look at this analogy by my friend: 'In some parts of the world big cats, competing with lions and tigers, chase down zebras for food in order to survive. Can we set a house-cat i.e. a domestic one, free in a jungle, to do the same thing? These are different types of cats, and they do not function in the same way. Just as these are two different cats that function in two different ways, these (ESL learners of India and the U.S.) are two different types of learners, and they function in different ways. English is not vital to survive in India. For migrant children of the U.S., it is a matter of survival. Is English a matter of survival in India?' No.

I heard from a learned Englishman saying, 'The idea of not using someone's first language i.e. mother tongue at all in an English class or in English medium school, is nothing other than linguistic theorizing and highbrow academic notions of how things should be.' According to him, using mother-tongue in English class is acceptable. However, as an English teacher, I used students' mother-tongue, occasionally, just to make them understand the meaning of a very difficult word. Generally, I used to give the context in which the word is used and asked them to decipher the meaning in the mother tongue. Since I was educated in the mother-tongue medium, I could easily understand my students' difficulties. Using intellect to theorize and talk about things is great. However, it is necessary to look at what happens on the ground.

The strategies that are to be adopted for teaching in a multilingual context are: translation, paraphrase, code-mixing, code-switching. Hence, multilingualism is equal to knowing things in different ways. These could be done effectively. Earlier, in English language teaching these kinds of measures were not in place. Only judicious use of the mother tongue was allowed, basically to promote the target language more. Whenever a difficult word or vocabulary item appeared, teachers were asked to show in action or facial gesture or by mimicking. Later, this procedure of verbal gyrations, looked awkward and tedious, on the part of the teacher. This realization has given leeway to giving the mother- tongue equivalent. That was the easiest way a student of a mother-tongue/regional medium could understand. Now, the same could be given in as many languages as the English teacher knows and the students understand. The alternation of languages reinforces one another and raise the understanding of content and language.

'Multilingualism in the world is the norm and the classrooms are no exception. The dynamic and flexible practices of multilingual teachers and learners in the classroom are referred to as translanguaging … It (translanguaging) is the means of communication employed by multilingual learners in multilingual learning settings.'[14]

1. Multilingualisms And Development- Selected Proceedings of the 11th Language Development Conference, New Delhi, India 2015, First Published 2017, D.P. Pattanayak, p.11

2. Language Policy and Education 2 in the Indian Subcontinent 3 Ajit K. Mohanty and Minati Panda, Springer International Publishing AG 2016 T. McCarty, S. May (eds.), Language Policy and Political Issues in Education, Encyclopaedia of Language and Education, DOI 10.1007/978-3-319-02320-5_37-1 pp.6-7

3. National Curriculum Framework (NCF) 2005, Publication Department- National Council for Educational Research and Training (N.C.E.R.T), Sri Aurobindo Marg New Delhi -110016, p.36

4. Ibid p.37

5. [NEP 2020, 4.12]

6. Krashen on Bilingualism https://youtu.be/9XR_fb1fv1g

7. https://citeseerx.ist.psu.edu/viewdoc/download?doi=10.1.1.20 .9706&rep=rep1&type=pdf

8. Priya Hosali 2000, The Butler English Form and Function, BR Publication, Ansari Road, Darya Ganj, New Delhi-110002 pp.90-91

9. Oxford English Dictionary 1933, p.8

10. R.A. Hall Jr, Pidgins and Creoles as Standard Languages, Sociolinguistics, Selected Reading, edited by J.B. Pride and Janet Holmes, 1972, printed in Great Britain by Hazell Watson & Viney Ltd. p.142

11. N. Krishnaswamy 1971, An Introduction to Linguistics for Language Teachers, Somaiya Publications Pvt Ltd, 172, Naigaum Cross Road, Dadar, Bombay-14DD. p.204

12. Rethinking monolingual instructional strategies in multilingual classrooms, Jim Cummins, Ontario Institute for Studies in Education, University of Toronto. *7-vol-10-no2-art-cummins monolingual ill-effects.pdf

13. N. Krishnaswamy 1971, An Introduction to Linguistics for Language Teachers, Somaiya Publications Pvt Ltd, 172, Naigaum Cross Road, Dadar, Bombay-14DD. p.212

14. https://www.tandfonline.com/doi/full/10.1080/07908318.2021.1979578?src=recsys

Assessment of ESL Acquisition through Examinations

Writing an Examination

Coming to writing, students have a problem. In the case of writing, they need to provide the context of what they are writing. That is, detailing the subject they are writing on. While speaking, they could use words sparingly, as the surrounding environment provides the context. A small gesture from the speaker, speaks volumes. Body language of the speakers also provides many signals. Students make many mistakes while writing. Teachers make an error analysis to grasp students, where they are in the learning process. Of course, errors are a common phenomenon, which is observed in the learning process. An error is slightly different from a mistake. As a matter of fact, errors made with carelessness are mistakes.

Error analysis

Many say foreign language or second language learning can be compared to a series of steps on a stair-case. Each step has its own difficulty. Even in mother tongue, learners often make errors. Hence, making errors means they are making an effort to learn. In each step learners exhibit errors characteristic of that particular step. The learner cannot move forward, until she is ready to cross the step. Often, we see a class-III learner that exhibits a kind of errors, while writing in the language or in doing mathematics sums, would overcome them by the time the learner reaches class-IV or V. Therefore, errors are indispensable in the learning process.

The errors typical of each step (in the learning) will disappear, when the learner passes to the next step. There will be a progressive elimination of the typical errors.

All the learners do not pass the stages at the same rate. Their speed differs (from an individual to an individual) but the order is the same for all. No amount of correction will move them to the next step, otherwise, they are ready for it. A teacher who is aware of this phenomenon may be likely to ask these questions: why should I take unnecessary strain to correct errors, if they are indispensable on the part of the learner? Why should I, as a teacher, waste my time in correcting the errors, when I cannot significantly eliminate their rate? The answer to such queries is to make the learner more responsible. By knowing psychology, a teacher must be able to provide opportunities for self-correction. It is the learner who has to learn, no amount of correction by the teacher can correct him.

Nevertheless, some teachers opine that teachers must correct every error in the learner's written work. And they should also provide them with correct answers, as the learners are incapable of correcting their errors. It is better for teachers to mark the errors than to correct them. Just to make a mention of error and number of errors in a page, at the side, is enough to give a cue for self-correction. Even if an overprotective teacher corrects her students' books, pointing all errors and their correct forms with a red pen, the learners do not or may not learn anything, as expected by the teacher. Also, the learner is likely to repeat the same mistakes, very often in the next assignment. An answer to a question or a piece of writing by the student, corrected with full red marks by the teacher, may develop a kind of tolerance (towards errors) in the student. Errors are not always evidence of faulty learning. As the teacher cannot prevent errors from occurring, as they are natural to the process of learning, the teacher needs only to mark errors in their written work. And allow the learners to correct the errors themselves. Students can correct by seeing the text or course-book where they went wrong. Better teach fishing than to give a fish, is a sound dictum in the teaching learning process. This is an overall theory on correcting errors.

However, sometimes teachers' correction-work helps. I was told by one professor that when he was a child, he used to write the spelling of the word: 'separate' wrong, by writing the spelling: 'seperate'. When he often made this mistake, in spite of the correction by the teacher, his teacher got annoyed and made the correction this way: sepArate. The correction was so glaring with a bold letter, he never forgot the corrected word in his lifetime. Later, he became an English professor. There are many ways and means. The teacher has to evolve in an innovative way. Like pointing the number of errors for self-correction at the margin for the student, is the minimalist way for the maximum benefit of the teacher. With the help of the textbook, the student has to find the correct spelling. When they take such strain to search for the word, they never forget its spelling. The teacher cannot do hard work for the student, it is the student that has to do. In the Discourse Oriented Pedagogy that is followed in Andhra Pradesh, Telangana and Kerala states of India, the correction and error-analysis is done by the English teacher on the blackboard. This they call editing. In a class, the students are divided into groups and each group is assigned to write a task. The teacher calls the group leader to read. In case of grammar or spelling-errors, editing the text of one student is done on blackboard by the teacher, so that all students could view what went wrong, where and why. Here, not an individual student, but all students would get a corrected version, at one go. Now, students could vet their written work/essays in their laptops/tablets using MS Word, Google docs. Through the Dictionary app, they could spell-check occasionally for self-correction. AI helps, if a problem arises with home assignments. Yet, to learn the English language a student's own effort is much needed.

Role of question-banks or guides

In India, competitive examinations are almost all in objective type. Subjective questions are not given, just to eliminate subjective discrimination by the evaluator. Since they are objective, students tend to learn from the question-banks available in the market that are written for the purpose. Instead, to get all-comprehensive knowledge on the subject, the students should be reading the text-books and other reference books. Pointing out this kind of faulty learning process, the National Education Policy 2020 writes, 'These exams (meaning to say competitive entrance examinations for joining in professional courses) also force students to learn a very narrow band of material in a single stream, rather than allowing the flexibility and choice that will be so important....'[1] That was the view of the National Education Policy 2020 with regard to competitive examinations. Students that study for general examinations also do not go by wide and flexible reading nowadays. They often read narrow question banks to pass the examinations. Hence, they do not acquire in-depth knowledge or understanding of the subject. There are many disadvantages in having these *bazaar* guides otherwise known as question banks for learning the English language. Since the textbooks do not change for years, these question banks are passed to new entrants to the class from the old students. As far as the English subject is concerned, these guides provide the meaning of each reading passage i.e. the lesson, in students' mother tongue or local language. As a result of that, students reading on their own and knowing or eliciting the meaning on their own would not happen. Sometimes, they read before the teacher starts the unit of the lesson. While the actual lesson reading they lose the kind of discovery value i.e. that they are making an effort by deciphering the meaning to what they read. Because, they know everything in their mother-tongue by reading the guide. This will impair the surprise value in their learning process. To understand how to comprehend a passage given in English, teachers of English take pains to set tasks for students. These plans become futile, as they already know the full lesson in their comfortable mother tongue/local language.

Language could be interpreted in several ways. The guide or question bank-setter is also a teacher, though the book is written for commercial purposes. Sometimes, his interpretation of the language items is slightly different from that of the teacher, who is actually teaching. This makes students a bit confused. Furthermore, the Board Examination Paper-Setters most often go by these easily made available guides with umpteen number of objective bits, as available resources to give in the question-paper. In a way this is a kind of encouragement to students to follow the question-banks.

Way back, the practice was, soon after the lesson was completed in the class, the teacher would ask students to write answers to questions on their own, on the lesson taught. This, usually was given as a home assignment. In those days, guides were not in the market. Teachers used to correct these home assignments at leisure and would find out where the fault lies: in their teaching or learning by the learners. That used to help them to rectify. Now, the home assignments are of no use. Invariably, students lift answers from the guides/question-banks to write on. English is not the only subject singled out in this manner. All subjects have question-banks/guides. So, the dependence has become permanent.

Years ago, subjects like mathematics, science, social sciences, English and Telugu were studied extensively. There were many reference books apart from the prescribed textbook for the class. That is in the case of high school and college. Now, most of the students have stopped searching for knowledge in varied sources. Instead, their only source has become the guide/question-banks that give sketchy and limited knowledge. In a way, this is all, examination-oriented era. Like earlier, if a student makes an effort in reading extensively and putting out the matter more elaborately, the examiner, who corrects the Board-Exam papers, would not find time to correct or read that lengthy answer. She or he goes by the answer key, where cut and dried points are provided as answers. The evaluator only searches for them in the written-matter and ticks them as the right ones. The student who provides that much stuff is good enough. The student that goes overboard with extra knowledge becomes more of a nuisance. Hence, the system of education would not provide a privilege for extensive reading.

However, of late, the core is enough --- this concept is gaining currency. The NEP 2020 says, 'All textbooks shall aim to contain the essential core material (together with discussion, analysis, examples, and applications) deemed important on a national level, but at the same time contain any desired nuances and supplementary material as per local contexts and needs.'[2] This is again an ideal. When only the core is provided, in the discussion part the teacher has to involves students. Because, to participate, a student needs to have some knowledge (content) on that particular subject and intellect on how to use it. Where does the student get the knowledge from? If it is from the Internet, it should be available to browse. If it is from various other reference books from the library, she or he must be interested in reading them. Hence, it is pains taking to involve students. Most of them do not participate in debates and discussions in the classroom, as they are culturally, attuned to teacher teaching. Moreover, they presume it is the teacher's duty to explain and for them to silently listen to.

Of course, the confident students that interact in the class possess English knowledge. Otherwise, they would not be confident. It is for the teacher to bring the shy students to speak. It needs a lot of patience. It needs proper formation of questions. They should be precise, clear and direct. Easy and comprehensible. Interesting questions should be asked to drive home, in their thinking a message or a vision or a guiding principle to grasp. Interaction between teacher and student, should lead to brainstorming on the part of the student. In a way, core- syllabus is good. Because, all students are not interested in going deep or horizontally to gain knowledge on the topic. But, if this becomes a habit, the content-based syllabus becomes totally redundant. Of course, that has already happened in many ways. When a student goes to post-graduation, she becomes incapable of collecting or gathering knowledge on her own. The knowledge around her digitally is a big heap. To browse, she needs lots of time. She cannot take it all unfiltered for her project. Sometimes, it is better to read hard-bound texts written by subject experts than some digitized wayward articles to naturalize or digest the content. It applies to English too. Those who would like to improve English, instead of going to digital platforms and getting tips, it is better to sit in a cozy corner with a hard copy of a novel or classical drama to read. The physical touch of the book, the silence, the print on the paper, the concentration of reading gives more grasp and personalisation. After all, did we forget climbing steps after we got to the escalators? No wonder old is gold. Downloadable Pdfs are invariably printable!

Perhaps, the NEP 2020 emphasized more on the basic core-competencies, because they are essential on any subject for all learners. If the content is more, the uninterested students get bored. For, as far as schools are concerned, the subjects to study are not optional. Hence, this way, core principles on each vital subject are desired to be learned by the student. Content-based texts have become redundant in this computer and internet-age, as knowledge regarding any subject is a click-away. Students could view video-lectures from eminent scholars on the subject from all over the world. However, when it comes to guides/question-banks, they do not provide an intellectual treatise on the subject. Their bare-minimal knowledge on the subject, especially a skill-subject like English, would not help. If it does help, it helps in making them get a pass mark. But for it, the student has to read what the guide maker provides. Even if it is not enjoyable to read from the guides, students' resort to, as an easy way out, to get marks. Sometimes, even some of the district education department's make minimum support material for slow-learners to read and pass the exam. This minimum-support material is easy to understand and it is like a guide/question-bank. This type of coaching culture is perpetuated, as students are promoted from one class to the other, not based on knowledge acquired, but on free-promotion policy of the government. Of course, promotion to the next class/standard has the criteria of attendance. Often this attendance is condoned for various reasons.

When I asked my ex-student (now working in an MNC) regarding the usefulness of question-banks, he said, 'I could say all these guides can help for grammar, but not for fluency of English language. As per my experience, fluency in English is possible by continuous interaction in English and correction by a coach. That will give confidence to learners and they will overcome English phobia.' He said guides are helpful in the "grammar aspect". This he said, because the question-banks carry extensive exercises on grammar items like: direct and indirect speech, active and passive voices, question tags, prep-phrases and so on and so forth. As an English teacher, while teaching grammar, I used to give my students two or three examples in the class, on each grammatical item. Students' prescribed workbooks would give another five sentences. That would not suffice to get a grasp on the grammar item or to use it for speaking. Another ex-girl student (who is holding a good post in Telangana State-Government) said, 'According to me workbooks which are given along with English text books are enough to help the students to learn English apart from teachers' teaching. Students do not need any questions-banks or guides which are sold in the market.' This girl was a very studious student while in school.

Ends- Justify- Means-Type of Examinations

'Board exams and entrance exams result in a coaching culture… replacing valuable time for true learning with excessive exam coaching and preparation…'[3], This is a statement of fact.

The situation is lamentable. But the choice before the student or teacher is limited. In this fast- paced technological world 'true learning' i.e. learning a subject thoroughly, in detail, and understanding it, is lacking. Many are content with a decent or satisfying job than to aspire to become a scientist like: Sir C.V. Raman or Jagadish Chandra Bose. Our education system, sadly, would not allow it. A teacher is assessed on her performance by the results students get in the Board-examination. Hence, it would be the goal and endeavour of the teacher to achieve that. The teacher may not teach the entire academic year in an examination-oriented way. Sincere teachers try all possible means to get the end result. Try to improve students' learning process. In any case, they also target the year-end - exam-result in the day-to-day world. At the fag end of the academic year i.e. last semester, the orientation of a teacher and student is, in the examination point of view. The last months are also part of the academic calendar to impart genuine learning to take place. However, that is being overruled by the exams.

For many students their strength lies in their question banks/guides (already published ones), where answers for all questions and objective grammatical and structural items are designed and given. The previous Board-examination papers with answers are available in them. Learning by rote the answers is an easy practice. The power of committing to memory by the children is tremendous. Many academicians disagree with rote-learning. They say it kills creativity. According to me, rote learning of poems in English, definitions of concepts in science, mathematics and certain paragraphs from a text to quote or for annotation, are all necessary. Removing totally rote learning impairs a child's memory. That is the reason as to why NEP 2020 accepted rote learning to a small extent but wanted pedagogy to evolve. NEP 2020 says, 'While learning by rote can be beneficial in specific contexts, pedagogy must evolve to make education more experiential, holistic, integrated, discovery-oriented, learner-centred, discussion-based, flexible, and, of course, enjoyable.'[4]

In India, most often Central or State Board examination marks are not the yardstick for selection into professional courses. The students have to appear for a common competitive examination to get a seat. This is one way good. Geeta Gandhi Kingdon, Professor of Education Economics at University College London (UCL) in her blog article pointed out: Exam boards (in India) mislead learning levels by awarding them (students) artificially inflated marks. 'The elation of stratospherically high marks must be tempered with the knowledge of the deception therein! All stakeholders … must oppose the malpractice of marks inflation…'[5], she asserted. Several studies on assessments in India have found that student assessment data is often artificially inflated and hence unreliable.[6] Taking the lacunae in the assessment of students in school-level, to correct the system, the National Education Policy (NEP) 2020 prioritizes assessments as a critical tool for improving quality of education.

1.   National Education Policy 2020, Ministry of Human Resource Development Government of India. p.16

2.   Ibid 4.28

3.   Ibid 4.32

4.   Ibid p.3

5.   https://timesofindia.indiatimes.com/blogs/toi-edit-page/hoodwinking-indias-children- exam-boards-mislead-on-learning-levels-by-awarding-them-artificially-inflated-marks/?source=app&frmapp=yes

6.   Pre Chapters final export updated 16.7.21 (dell.org)

Chapter–15

Covid-19 Pandemic-Innovative English Teaching

In Covid-19 pandemic affected years (2020-22), English teachers heavily relied on technology. Those teachers that are not tech-savvy also learnt how to use it. It is the sheer imperative that drove them to learn tech-devices to teach. There are many hidden aspects of the teaching-learning process that came to the forefront. One of them is an English teacher's pronunciation. The pronunciation of most of the teachers is accented with their L1 to a great extent. Insisting on pronunciation to be correct as native English speaker- like, is too ambitious. But towards that end, if the teacher and students worked, at least, they may attain an accent-neutral. However, to have a good pronunciation would be an asset in the long run. For, it is beneficial, as it is intelligible all over the world. Otherwise, a listener should strain himself or herself to understand what the speaker is saying. There is no denying the fact that oral organs of articulation are attuned to pronounce certain syllables in a certain way, according to one's mother tongue, right from childhood. Hence, the syllabification and stress used in English differs with that of the speaker's native language. This is the problem mostly with the older generation. In India, one could easily make out, from which provincial state or region a person comes from by his or her way of speaking English, but not by looks. Of course, it is a world-wide phenomenon in all countries. But of late, in the younger generation of Indians, this problem of regional accent is not much. Many urbanites are good at catching pronunciation and grammar through exposure.

During the Covid-19 pandemic years, teachers innovatively used technology and devised their own teaching materials of English. A Telangana state government school teacher said that he had developed ICT material and e-contents like Graphics, Audio, Text, Video, Animation, etc. This e-content is made available on the Internet as well as in the form of CDs and DVDs. Many apps are also available... e-patasala is one of the best apps for students, teachers, and parents. Radio can also be used as a good resource.[1]

In Telangana Government Schools to improve students' English Education Expos are conducted. An EXPO is the collection of education-related interactive materials and their display in the public domain. Under EXPO, the language learning activities include pronunciation, sentence framing, Jolly Phonics, dictionary use, English stories, and adjectives. For the students to learn the adjectives and their usage, they are asked to give labelling before their name using adjectives. Teachers say through the Phonics app, children have improved their reading skills. They could also identify tricky words and correct spelling. It has enhanced the writing capacities of students, say the teachers.[2]

Earlier, the use of a dictionary came under 'study skill' in English language teaching. To open the page for finding a particular word's meaning was taught. How to use the dictionary was not known to students then. Nowadays, dictionaries are on mobile phones. Opening the page, turning and tracing the word-meaning, has become redundant. In the Dictionary app word-meaning comes along with pronunciation, an option that can be used. The animated English stories are available on social media platforms. Vocabulary and grammar teaching videos are available on the internet taught by experts. There is no dearth of teaching, at present, besides the English teacher's teaching. To improve reading capabilities and correct spelling depend on students' own effort. Otherwise, the acquisition of English has ample scope compared to the pre-digital era. Globalization and digitisation have empowered English learning capabilities. Thanks to the advancement of technology. This technology plays a level-playing field. For, it caters to all types of learners. By nature, some are rapid-learners and some are slow-learners. Technology caters to both. On the other hand, the new technology: Artificial Intelligence (AI) and Chatbots are of elite preserve. Let us see what ChatGPT is all about.

New technology

The new technology, ChatGPT, is supposed to be very advanced. It was only released last year. Students can make use of ChatGPT or Chatbot for solutions to the language related write-ups. Technology is useful to make things easier. Students' excessive work-burden gets lessened with ChatGPT. Nevertheless, it has huge implications. If students start using ChatGPT for creative-writing, it would scuttle their own imagination and individual autonomous freedom of thought. If they use it for knowledge, the Artificial Intelligence (AI that's used in Chatbot) will enhance their knowledge and the pace of generation of it. Hence, the limits and capabilities of Artificial Intelligence (AI) should be known to students.

The ChatGPT is a disruptive technology, in the sense that it will hamper students' own thinking and the principle of discovery in studying. After much use of it, students are likely to give up their own thought process. For, by getting absorbed in the multitudes of thoughts and ideas produced by AI. Moreover, it is said that ChatGPT is available, merely, in about twenty languages of the world. As a consequence, the ChatGPT is likely to degenerate the numerous other languages in the world. The poor students, who could not afford them or are incapable of using them, will lag behind.

Besides technology, English language as an enabler

There are some school-headmasters, who are strong proponents of the English medium. According to a headmaster in Telangana state government run school: 'gaining knowledge in English is a progressive step. It will help in a child's all-round development. It is better to learn English earlier on than late in life, as it helps fluency to talk or to write. The child could easily face the 21st century challenges by knowing English. So, therefore parents from economically weaker sections also would like to join their children in the English medium schools. To cater to the demands of the parents and students, the state-run Telugu medium schools both primary and higher levels (in A.P. and Telangana states) are slowly turning into English medium schools.'[3]

All state government-run schools in India either have English as a subject from primary school or the medium of instruction. Almost all Indians know the benefit of knowing the English language. In India people do not despise English as a colonial legacy. In fact, they are using it to their advantage. Whereas there are various theories floating around the world on the English hegemony. Some of them are scathing. These theories are:

1. English is promoting monolingual culture.

2. English imperialism

3. Native-speakerism.

4. The others say: whatever English they speak in their countries and the manner they learn according to their context and culture should be accepted. To them. there is no 'one' English. There are many Englishes.

There are native, post-colonial varieties of English in the countries the British ruled. They are not pidgins and creoles, but they are of full-fledged English. The only difference is, in accent and articulation. Indian-English, Malaysian-English, Thai-English, Chinese-English, Singaporean-English, Nigerian-English etc. differ with the native-speakers viz. the British and American-English. By encouraging or by accepting Englishes, the natives are accepting plurality. There are arguments on both sides i.e. the native and non-native speakers of English. Some of the debates and discussions are given at the "Conclusion".

Latest on-going Debates and Discussions on English

1. English Imperialism

Robert Phillipson is the vociferous proponent of this theory: English Imperialism. Phillipson (1992) challenged the following five inter-related assumptions underlying much of English language teaching (ELT) in global contexts:

i. English is best taught monolingually.

ii. The ideal teacher of English is a native speaker.

iii. The earlier English is taught, the better the results.

iv. The more English is taught, the better the results.

v. Standards of English will decline if other languages are used for any significant amount of instructional time.[4]

Auerbach (1993) elaborates on these assumptions in the context of teaching English to adults in North America. She argues that although exclusive use of English in teaching ESL is typically seen as a natural and common-sense practice, there is, in fact, minimal pedagogical evidence supporting this approach. She reviews evidence showing that 'L1 and/or bilingual options are not only effective but necessary for adult ESL students with limited L1 literacy or schooling and that the use of students' linguistic resources can be beneficial at all levels of ESL'.[5] Like Phillipson, she highlights the fact that the monolingual principle is rooted in a particular ideological perspective which serves to reinforce inequities in the broader society.

While I entirely agree with what Auebach said, about adult learners in her context of North America, in the Indian context, it appears, both adults and children need a bilingual option, for understanding the English language. Though they are quite capable in their L1, when it comes to English as a second language, the skill in L1 would not get transferred seamlessly. In all states of India, the regional languages are spoken. State language is prevalent in all spheres of life. There is no need to interact in English for the common people in their daily lives. Hence, spoken English is very less. After all, a language is learnt in spoken form first and then only in written form. Very few have a reading habit to gain the language. For Auerbach, North America is an English-speaking country. In that environment her adult learners also get exposed to English in day-to-day affairs. In India, there is no such scope. Therefore, both young and adult learners of ESL need L1 support. As she said, students' linguistic resources could be beneficial at all levels of ESL. The "inequities in the broader society", she mentioned because of monolingual English, have already taken roots in India. Paradoxically, to have a level playing field, not going by Phillipson theories, many are opting voluntarily for English. Even the poorest in India perceive English to be a leveller in the society. Though all Indians love and respect their mother-tongues, they all would like to have English as a good add-on.

'Is English all we need?', Phillipson questions and then he adds, 'English is now marketed as a language that everyone needs and that all should learn. This is one of the myths of global English. It is blithely proclaimed as the lingua franca of science, of business, … of international understanding as though no other languages serve such purposes.'[6]

Some academicians opine, what is meant by linguistic imperialism in Phillipson's terms could be the imposition of English in primary schools, in officially English-speaking countries, that were former colonies, like Ghana. These countries bar students from accessing higher education when their English is considered improper. But, primary schools around the world have many reasons to fail, not on the account of the English language alone. However, according to Phillipson in Denmark, 'The systematic coverage of a range of reports commissioned by the government or business is complemented by examples of

English-only blindness, a sickness that has infected all levels of the education system.'[7] That state of affairs mentioned has to be condemned.

Phillipson's other arguments:

i.   The global teaching of English was an act of linguistic imperialism.

ii. Its prominence in global language education has effectively undermined the rights of other languages and marginalized the opportunities that should exist for widespread multilingual education.

iii. The spread of English has accompanied the political and economic intentions of English-speaking nations to conquer other countries.

iv. English endangers in the non-English speaking countries their local cultural ideals, ways of life and indigenous languages.

All these arguments were countered by Anne Burns. She says the above arguments of Phillipson, 'have also provoked a number of criticisms, among which are: i). making teachers feel unnecessarily guilty about teaching English, and ii). adopting a patronizing attitude towards developing countries by assuming they are incapable of making their own decisions about language choice',[8] in any case, India does not give excessive importance to English but recognises it as a language to be learnt for better opportunities.

2. Native Speakers Teaching English

Who are the best speakers of a language (be it any language)? It is, of course, the native speakers. Noam Chomsky said a native speakers' language cannot be challenged. For, the native speaker acquires the language right from childhood by his or her surroundings. If you are a Telugu person living in Telugu speaking states (Andhra or Telangana) obviously you learn Telugu to speak well. Because it is your L1. You are an expert user of it. Nobody says you are making mistakes in that language. That is the advantage of being a native speaker. On the other hand, if you are speaking English, there is scope for some expert user of English to point out something wrong in your English. Because, English is not an acquired language for you right from the beginning, but a learnt language later in life. Though while learning English, some amount of acquisition takes place, but that does not make you a native user. Moreover, native speakers know the nuances of the language better. That being the case, should a native speaker alone teach the language? If you are a Telugu, Tamil, Hindi or Gujarati, you could speak your language fluently without any mistakes. But can you teach your language to others that are not of your language? The answer is: yes and no. Some can teach, some cannot. For teaching the language or teaching any subject, you need expertise. The expertise to teach the language is either innate or by training. 'It is not difficult to see that many scholars now prefer the term "expert user", which refers to "a proficient speaker of the language, regardless of whether it is their first language or not. Others have gone so far as to disclaim native speaker ownership of English as it is used in the 21st century.[9] I agree with the theory that an expert user is one that is a proficient speaker of a language, though not it is his L1. Practically, I have seen some Muslim teachers (though their mother-tongue is Urdu) teach Telugu language in schools and colleges to Telugu children in Andhra Pradesh and Telangana. For, these teachers grew up Telugu-speaking and learnt Telugu as a state language. Hence, they are well-versed.

However, in the case of English, native English speakers are scarce in non-native lands. Whatever available, they may not have the inclination to teach. The ESL teachers working in India, learnt English as a second language and know the troubles of learning. Therefore they could teach with a better understanding of the subject. For this reason they are suitable to teach. When they teach, learners can understand better. Where a learner gets a doubt is, in their experiential orbit. If a native speaker were to teach, she would have a problem in understanding learners' mind and thought-process. As far as the learner is concerned, the first hurdle for her/him is the teacher's pronunciation. Next comes the nuances of culture. They cannot understand the native teacher's idioms, jokes, wit and sarcasm etc. It looks alien to them. In India, English is taught bilingually in most of the schools. To make children understand English to English is not possible for the simple reason that both the teacher and the student are not up to that level. In any case, India may not foresee such a situation (English to English) in all schools. The average Indian is comfortable with a bilingual or a multilingual method. These bi/multilingual students are no less. They have proved themselves best in their lives. Widdowson 2003 finding builds a convincing case for that fact. He says, …

'how English develops in the world is no business whatever of its native speakers in England, the United States, or anywhere else. They have no say in the matter, no right to intervene or pass judgment. They are irrelevant. Even in the area of teaching, native speakers no longer enjoy the monopoly they once used to hold.'[10]

Thornbury 2006 writes 'One reason is that the native speaking teacher hasn't learnt the language in a classroom context, which is where many learners learn English and therefore "are not as well- positioned to teach it".'[11] This may be argued in another way. All educated native speakers learn their language as L1 in their formative years in their primary schools. All English-speaking countries ensure primary education. However, the problem comes when these educated English-teachers try teaching in non-English speaking countries. There they need to understand the classroom context of the learners. If they are patient enough, they could teach. But to consider that the native English –speakers are the custodians of the language, would only restrict the language from spreading. It is a conservative thinking. Being liberal and generous would ensure the language to fly high. Widdowson 2003 states, "to grant such custody of language is necessary to arrest its development and so undermine its international status".[12]

The ideology of native speakers' ownership of language is more seriously questioned today than ever before. For, English has spread over many former colonies of the British and the U.S. At present most of the countries, though independent and have their native languages, still continue English as the second language. In the case of the not colonized countries, people are learning English as a third or foreign language. This is especially because English has become the global lingua franca. In these countries the way people speak differs with that of native speakers of English. This is because the people, while speaking English, switch to the sociolinguistic realities of their land. Their vocabulary, grammar, and pronunciation are distinctive and differs with the standard variety. Finally, it is the considered opinion of many that wherever English is taught as a second language (ESL), the teaching community has to arise from it. At least at the primary and secondary level of teaching English, the teacher should have familiarity with the learners and their problems. Being a native speaker of English is not enough to teach that language. It is the teaching methodology and grasp of students' needs regarding the language, are necessary.

3. Monolingual English Classroom

Monolingual ESL classes use only English and no other language. These are basically English-alone classrooms in order to improve the English language. Apparently, they follow Immersion or Direct Method in teaching English. The principle behind it was, as there is no scope for English language outside the classroom, it has to be within the class. However, while studying the English language, the use of learners' L1 or any other familiar native language would enhance their understanding is the belief of the opponents of monolingual teaching. 'English does not stand alone… English needs to find its place along with other Indian languages in different states'… was the stated view in the NCF 2005.[13] Even in the recent NEP 2020, the same is reiterated.

Douglas Brown 2007 states that 'learning a foreign language also means learning a new culture, …: It is apparent that culture, as an ingrained set of behaviours and modes of perception, becomes highly important in the learning of a second language. A language is a part of a culture, and a culture is a part of a language: the two are intricately interwoven so that one cannot separate the two ….'[14] Crossing the cultural boundaries, English in India has become like one of the Indian languages. It is no more a foreign language to Indians. Earlier, in the pre-independent years of India and later, soon after independence to the country, English was a foreign language. But now it is like one of the Indian languages and remains so in India. Though English mannerism varies from the native Indian one, Indians are good at using alternate cultures as per appropriate situations. After globalization of the Indian economy in 1991, with the entry of market forces, the importance of English has increased. Many youngsters are opting to learn in the English medium. They think it is profitable. With the onslaught of English, Indian languages took a back-seat. English has become the most dominant language in the world. In India it is a big language and in comparison, Indian languages have become small, especially in the education field. But of course not in normal life. Therefore a fear of psychosis has crept in on the vulnerability of Indian languages that are under attack by the dominance of English. Already with the monolingual English medium schools spreading, there is disappearance of rich and strong Indian languages in the education curriculum. Apart from that many children are unable to understand what is taught to them in English.

The eventual fading away of Indian languages within the realm of education is a worrying factor. This, K. David Harrison 2007 had aptly pointed out: 'Language disappearance is an erosion or extinction of ideas, of ways of knowing, and ways of talking about the world and human experience.'[15] If Indian languages slowly disappear in future, 'our rich patrimony of human cultural heritage, including myth and belief systems, wisdom, poetry, songs, and epic tales',[16] which we have built over centuries, would vanish. Once lost it is difficult to reclaim.

All in all, the atmosphere in the country is not conducive for the growth of the mother tongue. English has overtaken the language of opportunity and status. This type of thinking regarding English has been brewing in society for a long time due to a variety of reasons. Nonetheless, most of the Indians that learnt English in India learnt through their mother tongue in a bilingual way. Prof Rama Kanth Agnihotri writes, 'The fact that all of us learnt our English through our own languages is evidence enough that there is no need for 'English only' classes.'[17]

'English is a popular language by historical accident rather than its linguistic superiority.' 'No language is superior or inferior to any other language.' … That kind of statement made by the linguists, although true, on the ground the situation is different in India. However, in India, though people love their mother tongues and are fluent in speaking them, they take a harder option of English for their children's education. In any case, in India quite differently a large-scale survey conducted across the country by Prof Agnihotri and Khanna in 1997 showed the result that 'even though people wanted to preserve their languages, they did wish to add English to their repertoire'.[18]

Anyhow, my personal experience of teaching monolingual English was received well only by studious and rapid learners. The others pleaded for mother-tongue/L1 use. I used to say, 'If I have to use your mother-tongue extensively in my English class, it will become another L1 class for you, not the L2 I am teaching you'. Those were the days of monolingual domination to encourage English learning. Nonetheless, judicious use of mother-tongue in English class is always acceptable. The extensive use of mother-tongue by some other teachers also was welcomed by learners. When the Board Examinations came, all fared equally well. This is all because the learning outcomes would not solely depend on how teachers teach. The outcomes depend on equal measure or more on how the students put in their effort to learn. Many students have their ways and means to write the examination to score high marks/grades, once they understand, as second language learners, what English language is all about.

4. Multilingualism

'The aim of English teaching (in India) is the creation of multilinguals who can enrich all our languages; this has been an abiding national vision. The multilingual perspective also addresses concerns of language and culture, and the pedagogical principle of moving from the known to the unknown,' says the NCF 2006 Position Paper on English. This vision is abiding; hence it is taken forward in NEP 2020.

In India Prof Ajit K Mohanty has done immense work in multilingualism. He says because of the formation of linguistic states in India (soon after Independence) the dominance of 'one' language i.e. the language spoken in the state has pushed the minor languages to the edge. In the Government, Judiciary and Market Place English is predominant. Private English medium schools are increasing every year. As a result, there is a push back of home language leading to push out from the major domains. As the students learn more English, the less the mother tongue and other local languages, they (those languages) are weakening. This, Professor Mohanty points out as the "subtractive effect". He emphasizes that: monolingual-English classrooms, Direct Method, No-Translation are not necessary to teach English. Supporting multilingual English classrooms, he opines, multilingual children are cognitively better i.e. their mental faculties work effectively. It is better to use "additive use" of English not subtractive to mother tongue or other languages.

In the English-alone class, learners do not participate much. For this you do not need any empirical evidence. To bring in one's own language is good. In your mother tongue, you learn to swim automatically like a fish in a pond. How fish take to water, children learn their mother tongue, so is the surrounding atmosphere. Whereas in English you are an amphibian. Hence use of multiple languages could be made more intentional and structured, Prof Mohanty opines. He also says multilingualism is a collaboration between the languages in society and in the classroom. It is not competition but collaboration. The similar view S.N. Sridhar in 2020 expresses: 'a multilingual language repertoire is not compartmentalized but integrated, with all the languages functionally complementing and interacting with one another.'[19]

The point to be noted here is, India is a multilingual country. English is only available to an average student in school in an English class alone. Whereas in the U.S. and U.K, since they are monolingual English-speaking countries, the ethnic minority languages of immigrants have no place. The liberal intellectuals have been trying to incorporate a child's home language to have an understanding of what is being taught. On the Indian side, multilingual teaching is needed because the student needs the support of familiar languages to understand English. Hence, there is a clarion call for multilingualism. That will increase the student's comfort level in the class. Arguing for multilingualism in the English classroom Prof Agnihotri writes, '…a pedagogy rooted in multilinguality that would ensure the emergence of a society that is marked not only for its happiness and peace but also for its justice, equality, liberty and care for others.'[20] The techniques that are used in a multilingual English classroom are code-switching and code-mixing. More than code-mixing, code-switching is useful in higher classes. Even for code-switching and code-mixing, one language with the other, the student must be efficient and confident in the language the student is using. Yet, 'while communicating most of the errors in other tongues by way of pronunciation, accent, and little bit of grammar tilt are overlooked for want of meaning the person is conveying. Spoken communication could afford these marginal errors in any language with impunity. More than pronunciation, for language use, pragmatics i.e. directness, politeness and deference in language are given importance.'[21] In any case, 'India needs English. Indian children should learn English but not at the cost of Indian languages.'[22]

5. Global Englishes (GE)

Language variations are common in any language. They differ from region to region. The Telugu spoken in Andhra differs from the Telangana region. Similarly, English spoken in the different parts of the U.K and the U.S. differs. These are called dialectal variations. However, English spoken in India, China, Thailand,

Malaysia etc. and all non-native English- speaking countries is different from the native variety, because of sociolinguistic reasons. Research on varieties of English is an on-going process. Debates on ideologies like: native-speakerism, monolingualism, English-imperialism, English-hegemony, World Englishes, Postcolonial Englishes are all done in intellectual circles. Robert Phillipson opines that monolingualism and mono-culturalism are not sustainable, as the world environment is multicultural and multilingual. Debates on Global Englishes have been taking place for a decade or more. English-speakers in non-native countries are seeking recognition of their varieties on par with the native English. According to Fan Fang, the Global Englishes paradigm serves as a promising response to the complexity of identity, interaction, use and instruction surrounding the English language. It is increasingly important to enhance teachers' knowledge base i.e. their specialized knowledge skills, competencies, and commitments vis-à-vis the changing needs of English Language Teaching (ELT). He points out the gap in the ELT today is largely focused on 'native' ideology. Awareness of Global Englishes (GE) is generally lacking in ELT practices. To him, exposure to varieties of English is needed.

The on-going discussion in academic circles is: why Englishes, why not English? On the topic of 'Global Englishes lens' Fan Fang, an Associate Professor in the College of Liberal Arts, Shantou University, China, in one of his teachers' webinars says 'the traditional teacher education programs do not talk much about the importance of Global English. Increasingly there is a demand for the inclusion of Global English Language Teaching (GELT). The advocates of the GELT are not asking for abandoning current theories of nativized English but seeking for the critical examination of the changing world of English i.e. Global English lens.'[23] Among the academic circles some are totally against English. They are the opponents of English imperialism, monolingual classrooms, only native teacher-teaching. Some others are a bit accommodative by seeking to include their varieties of English i.e. Global Englishes in teaching.

In Trinity College, London, a webinar was conducted. There the acceptability of pronunciation (in English)) in different parts of the world was not found fault with. In fact it was stated by one of the panellists, "Incorporating World Englishes into the curriculum does not mean removing native varieties from English classes or replacing them with what, sometimes, people mistakenly believe are less-perfect ones; it rather means enriching the available repertoire. It is a different way of looking at the language, a more inclusive, pluralistic and accepting way than the traditional, monolithic British-centred approach."[24]

The speakers of the English language now are '—mostly former colonies of English-speaking empires. These areas also represented the largest constituency of English language learners and users in the world: In these areas, hundreds of millions of people learned English as a second language and used it in a vast range of important domains, such as education, administration, legislation, law, technology, literature, and the media on a daily basis. Here, English was taught by teachers who were themselves non-native speakers.'[25] In India, China, Thailand, Malaysia and Singapore we find Indian, Chinese, Thai, Malaysian and Singaporean varieties of English. As long as people of these countries speak English within their country, it is alright. But globally it becomes a problem. The kind of English they speak is unintelligible to others. Hence, native speaker emulation is necessary. But how a large number of non-native speakers in the world can adopt native speakers' English—is the question raised by many academicians. For, native speakers have their own kind of vocabulary and local realities, which are different from the non-natives.

India is a multilingual country. The English accent of a Tamilian differs from the Hindi-speaking one. One argument is that Global Englishes promotes diversity. Streamlining everything (all types of Englishes) is no good. For instance, Indians, Chinese, Thai, Malaysian and Singaporeans citizens that remain in their own country and rarely have a chance to use Standard English need not learn by standard norms. Local variety is relevant to the context and intelligible to in the context. However, the counter argument goes that learning the standard variety of English would serve in the local as well as global contexts. As a teacher of English, one should be a role-model for students. That means, an English teacher should strive to teach towards the Standard one. That will be for both local and Global purposes.

6. Translanguaging

Teachers often see how learners are discussing among themselves the task given in English, in their L1/local language. They read the text in English and discuss it in another language either their mother tongue or regional language. This is called translanguaging. In the urban areas children speak more than two languages. They are multilingual. They can make use of them as and when necessary. 'Today's populations increasingly need translingual awareness, as they develop a complex mosaic of multilingual and multicultural communicative competences, repertoires and language resources. In schools too, bilingual and multilingual students need to be allowed to draw upon these resources, rather than being restricted to the use of the one or two languages authorized in the school setting.'[26] The dictionary meaning of translanguaging is: 'the practice of encouraging the seamless use of all languages spoken by the students and teacher rather than enforcing separation between the home language of students and the language of instruction. Translanguaging in the classroom involves finding cognates (related forms) and translating, but also means allowing group work in the students' language of choice. To say in simple terms teachers use translanguaging as a scaffold to link knowledge in the language of instruction i.e. English to the home language or L1. In other words, translanguaging means '… originally described by Williams 2002, referring to the alternation of two languages to reinforce each other and raise both understanding of content and language.[27]

For instance, to put it clearly, in a translanguaging class, the teacher speaks English and students take notes in any chosen language. The pair-work and group discussions in the language of their choice and negotiate the meaning of the text or task given. However, the text for discussion is in English. Students can plan in any language but the presentation has to be in English. In a multilingual country this kind of leverage should be given to learners. One may get a doubt as to what is the difference between translanguaging and interlanguage. The difference between them mainly is, interlanguage is used for the grammatical system that a learner creates in the course of learning another language. It shows that the learner is evolving and grasping rules.

One may wonder why all these language concepts; would it not suffice for monolingual or bilingual teaching of English in India? As the country is progressing, mobility of people from region to region has increased. More and more people have become multilingual. Hence, '...as English teachers we need to produce students who understand why linguistic diversity is a resource for creativity and cognition, who value all the languages that they speak, and who recognise the paucity of 'English only'.[28]

1. RISE AND SHINE, *Insights of new age school leaders,* Government of Telangana, School Education Department, p-75, SCHOOL LEADERSHIP ACADEMY, STATE COUNCIL OF EDUCATIONAL RESEARCH AND TRAINING, TELANGANA NATIONAL CENTRE FOR SCHOOL LEADERSHIP - NIEPA - NEW DELHI

2. Ibid. p.80

3. Ibid. p.140

4. Rethinking monolingual instructional strategies in multilingual classrooms, Jim Cummins, Ontario Institute for Studies in Education, University of Toronto. *7-vol-10-no2-art-cummins monolingual ill-effects.pdf p.225

5. Ibid. p.225

6. Phillipson, 2017, pp. 315-316

7. https://cbswire.dk/speakers-corner/becoming-language-less-world-citizens/

8. Anne Burns, 'Is English a form of linguistic imperialism?' 10 April 2013 - 14:51 (https://www.britishcouncil.org/voices-magazine/english-form-linguistic-imperialism)

9. Farid Ghaemi, Department of English, Karaj Branch, Islamic Azad University, Karaj, Iran) Amin M. Mostajeran, Tarbiat Modares University, Tehran, Iran- - The Fallacy of an Epistemic Break: a Case for Epistemic Realism—The Journal Of English As An International Language—Volume 10-Issue-1, 2015 VOLUME, pp. 93-94 *English_Language_Education_Situation_in.pdf

10. Ibid (Widdowson 2003, p. 43)

11. Ibid (Thornbury, 2006, p. 141)

12. Ibid (Widdowson, 2003, p. 43)

13. National Curriculum Framework (NCF) 2005, Publication Department-National Council for Educational Research and Training (N.C.E.R.T), Sri Aurobindo Marg New Delhi -110016, p.39

14. Teaching Language and Content in Multicultural and Multilingual Classrooms, CLIL and EMI Approaches, Palgrave Macmillan, p.321

15. K. David Harrison. (2007). "When Languages Die: The Extinction Of The World's Languages And The Erosion Of Human Knowledge". When Languages Die: The Extinction Of The World's Languages And The Erosion Of Human Knowledge. https://works.swarthmore.edu/fac-linguistics/50 When Languages Die_ The Extinction Of The Worlds Languages And T.pdf

16. Ibid

17. RAMA KANT AGNIHOTRI MULTILINGUALITY AND THE TEACHING OF ENGLISH IN INDIA, Academia, Accelerating the world's research. RKA_EFL__article-with-cover-page-v2.pdf

18. Ibid

19. A.K. Mohanty YouTube-video – online talk excerpt

20. RAMA KANT AGNIHOTRI MULTILINGUALITY AND THE TEACHING OF ENGLISH IN INDIA, EFL Journal 1:1 January 2010. ©2010 The English and Foreign Languages University.

21. Ibid

22. Ibid

23. https://www.youtube.com/live/eP1V80IofnA?si=tx18AIlyZgMHJ6cc

24. Claudia Schiavon and Alan Hall presented on '"Proper" English for a proper future - exposing Young Learners to World Englishes' at the Future of English

Language Teaching Conference 2020. https://resources.trinitycollege.com/teachers/english_language/webinars/proper-english-for-a-proper-future-exposing-young-learners-to-world-englishes

25. S.N. Sridhar- To appear in *Being and Becoming a Bilingual,* ed by Rajesh Sachdeva and Rama Kant Agnihotri. Delhi: Orient Swan (2020). INDIAN MULTILINGUALISM: ACQUISITION AND IMPLICATIONS

26. 11th Language & Development Conference 221, James Simpson, Translanguaging in the contact zone: Language use in superdiverse urban areas- H. Coleman (ed.). 2017. *Multilingualisms and Development.* London: British Council. ISBN 978-0-86355-840-5 (Canagarajah 2013)

27. Joana Duarte (2020) Translanguaging in the context of mainstream multilingual education, International Journal of Multilingualism, 17:2, 232-247, DOI: 10.1080/14790718.2018.1512607 p.240

28. (Janks 2009, 11-12)' James Simpson, Translanguaging in the contact zone: Language use in superdiverse urban areas- H. Coleman (ed.). 2017. *Multilingualisms and Development.* London: British Council. ISBN 978-0-86355-840-5

Acknowledgements

I express my sincere gratitude to the Secretary, Shri. Ch. Ramana Kumar M.Sc., B.Ed, Telangana Residential Educational Institutions Society (TREI Society), Hyderabad, for having given an encouraging endorsement on my book written and also duly commenting on the usefulness of the book both to teachers of English language and the enthusiasts of English education for reading.

I am deeply indebted to Prof (Retd) Paul Gunashekar and Prof (Retd) V. Sasikumar of English and Foreign Languages University (EFLU), Hyderabad, for their magnanimous words of encouragement on the utility of the book to the teachers and the general public. My respectful thanks to Dr P. Jani Reddy, Lecturer, Govt. District Institute of Education and Training (DIET), Ranga Reddy, Vikarabad, for his generous praise and appreciation of the book.

I also thank all my colleagues, who worked with me teaching English as a second language in the schools for their inputs. I thank all my students that helped me in framing some of the structures in the book. My special thanks to Ruksana and Ganesh Nathi for their input in writing i.e. filled in a questionnaire prepared for the purpose. Last but not the least, I also thank my family members for their unstinted support.

Annexure

I have given a questionnaire to two of my students, now grown-up and professionally well-placed. The answers they have written and mailed; I am placing here as they are with typos:

Student-1

A girl, who studied in a regional medium school. She studied English as a third language. In Telugu-speaking states of both Andhra Pradesh and Telangana, English is the third language. In these two states, there is a three-language formula. The first language is Telugu/Urdu, the second language is Hindi, the third is English. This girl, is now a government employee.

Questionnaire

1. **A brief description on advantages of studying in regional/ Telugu medium (as you have studied) in comparison to English medium-educated children.**

    Ans: Studying in regional language (Telugu) made understanding of subjects easy and effortless. Understanding Concepts and topics thoroughly became easy and as a result it always took less time for me to study and practice the same Subjects. Science subjects like physics, chemistry, Biology are concept oriented and one needs to develop interest in them by understanding them and by experimenting. Rote learning would not work here. Studying in my regional language made these concepts clear for me. Languge is a means to express ones opinions, concepts, ideas and discuss them or to ask questions. Expressing the same in a foreign language would have become a barrier in itself to communicate. I had the comfort of communicating in regional language and thus my main focus remained on learning the subject rather than struggling with communication or making grammatically correct sentences. I never had any hindrances to talk to my teachers, understand what they are explaining and discussing the same with my fellow students.

2. **A brief description indicating your feelings (along with incidents, if any, being faced at person-to-person level or face to face, while you met people i.e. while travelling or while you joined English medium classes in college or experiences in work sphere, as a disadvantage of not knowing English enough to tackle the situation.**

    Ans: I have never repented for not joining a English medium school because even the regional language medium schools offer English subject learning. We are taught Grammer and all the basics needed to understand and converse in English. The only difference is with the amount of practice. English medium students get more opportunities to practice and we get a little lesser opportunity. Learning and using some good set of vocabulary and continuous usage in day to day life is the mantra for us to excel in English Languahe. The one time I faced difficulty of not knowing English enough is during my transition from telugu medium to English medium during my intermediate. It took 5-6 months for me to learn all the technical terms in English. All my initial learning was in telugu and so I needed to know the technical terms in both telugu and English to make myself well acquainted with the subject. I had to work extra hard during this time. But once I mastered the terminology it again was a cake walk.

    The only drawback which I still find with not studying in English medium is I cannot converse very comfortably in English though I can fully understand the language. being English medium.

3. **A brief description on the transition from school (Telugu Medium) to college (English Medium) in order to cope with textbooks (being in English)**

    Ans: The transition from Telugu medium to English medium would seem sudden and drastic for any student just like any major life event. Whole text books would change from comfortable and well aquinted language i.e telugu to English which will puzzle the students. We can become comfortable only after learning the technical jargon in both English and regional language. Once if we are done learning the technical terminologies, we can understand the Concepts easily. But this is possible only with the gradual use of these terms and with day to day reading and writing. It will take some time, patience and effort to cope with the new change.

4. **A brief description on emotional or psychological barriers you had faced in communicating with the English speaking initially.**

   Ans: A constant fear of making some mistake in my communication also leads to fear of being insulted. This along with being shy has been the biggest barrier to talk in English in the first place.

5. **Have you ever had any regret for studying in your mother tongue medium later in life, when you encountered people that studied in English medium? A brief analysis**

   Ans: I have never regretted for being a student of Telugu medium. I had to put some extra effort for 5-6 months during my transition from telugu medium to English medium. After this I found myself at par with other English medium students and I was also equally capable of understanding the subjects. I was capable of expressing the same through reading and writing.

6. **Having studied in Telugu medium, do you advise any youngster in India to study in Telugu/mother tongue medium? If your answer is: 'Yes'-Why? if it is: 'No'-Why not?**

   Ans: Yes, I would advise youngsters to study in Telugu/ mother tongue medium for their primary education. Studying in mother tongue will help them understand concepts and subject well. Students are less burdened with studies as they need not mug up whole syllabus for the sake of Examinations without knowing the essence of real learning. Telugu can simplify learning, understanding and as a result studies become fun and enjoyment. Students can slowly transform to English medium later for higher education.

7. **Your thoughts on youngsters shifting to English medium nowadays. Do you think, Telugu as a language is being neglected in India?**

   Ans: Yes, Telugu is being neglected in India like most other regional languages. Younger generation Is wholly shifting towards English medium for persuing their education and as a result Telugu or any other languages has just become a subject to pass.

8. **Your thoughts on the depletion of Telugu medium schools in number in both Telugu speaking-states. Write briefly what would be the result or consequences of this shift in Telugu Medium to English Medium result in?**

Ans: Depletion of Telugu medium schools is mainly due to a perception of parents that English medium is better. Parents as a result are wanting their kids to persue education in English medium schools only. This is resulting in depletion of Telugu medium schools at a faster pace. When Telugu is taught just as a subject, students attention will be just on passing that subject. And it might not create love and interest on language as such. As a result students might not have fluency in reading and writing Telugu. They might not explore older books in Telugu which are rich of ideologies, culture and knowledge of regional places. As a result the age old customs, ceremonies, traditions might also fade away with the language.

9. **Just mention how did you feel about the English subject while in school----Easy? Difficult? If easy – in what way? If difficult-in what way? Because of grammar? Or because of spelling? Or because of sentence construction/ comprehension/ communicative skills? Any suggestions to tackle.**

Ans: English was one of my favorite subjects in school. English is easy because of Grammer. Practicing English and correcting sentences grammatically was more fun. Learning by enjoying is the only way to not making a monster out of English.

10. **What is your opinion on English Question Banks/Guides sold in the market? Do you think they are helpful to students, apart from teachers teaching? Or are they harming the interest of the student (because they give the entire lesson in Telugu version, so that the interest to know what is in the lesson, while the teacher is teaching, is lost)?**

Ans: According to me work books which are given along with English text books are enough to Help the students to learn English apart from teachers teaching. Students doesn't need any question banks or guides which are sold in market

Name: Ruksana

Student-2

A boy, who had his school-studies in regional-Telugu-medium. Now, he is well-placed in an MNC (Multi-National Corporation)

Questionnaire

1. **A brief description on advantages of studying in regional/ Telugu medium (as you have studied) in comparison to English medium-educated children.**

   Ans: Studying in the mother tongue is advantageous to the child's development. A child can understand concepts and subjects better and they can express themselves more fluently when taught in their mother tongue.

2. **A brief description indicating your feelings (along with incidents, if any, being faced at person-to-person level or face to face, while you met people i.e. while travelling or while you joined English medium classes in college or experiences in work sphere, as a disadvantage of not knowing English enough to tackle the situation.**

   Ans: When I was in my B.Tech first year, I am unable to understand high vocabulary in English class because my lecturer used to teach in English only even though 20% students were from Telugu medium, fear to ask lecturer to explain in regional language and it is not a right thing to disturb every one because of majority students were from English Medium background. One day I got up and asked but few of my classmates make fun of me.

   Second incident happened in my 3rd year, I registered my name for paper presentation and short listed for next level, finally I tried to express my views in English but not delivered in proper way and no guidance on "how to express".

   I have a dissatisfaction while interacting with foreign delegates even though working in MNC company.

   After these incidents I started to guide everyone who are surrounded (Neighbours and Relatives) me to join in English medium.

3. **A brief description on the transition from school (Telugu Medium) to college (English Medium) in order to cope with textbooks (being in English)**

Ans: During switchover phase students alone won't get interest to read text books in English, it leads to low performance in their subjects as compare to earlier, but with guidance of lecturers it can overcome and align with text books in English.

4. **A brief description on emotional or psychological barriers you had faced in communicating with the English speaking initially.**

answered in Question No-2.

5. **Have you ever had any regret for studying in your mother tongue medium later in life, when you encountered people that studied in English medium? A brief analysis**

answered in Question No-2.

6. **Having studied in Telugu medium, do you advise any youngster in India to study in Telugu/mother tongue medium? If your answer is: 'Yes'-Why? if it is: 'No'-Why not?**

Ans: I won't advise youngster to study in Telugu Medium. Any professional career starts with English only, then why& what should we do with Telugu medium?

7. **Your thoughts on youngsters shifting to English medium nowadays. Do you think, Telugu as a language is being neglected in India?**

Ans: Every regional language is neglecting in India because of people have a fear in their child's career get badly affected by regional language and they may not be competing with English medium students.

8. **Your thoughts on the depletion of Telugu medium schools in number in both Telugu speaking-states. Write briefly what would be the result or consequences of this shift in Telugu Medium to English Medium result in?**

Ans: Consequences:

we couldn't protect our language; the Telugu community will lose its presence. We will lose our identity. Next generation will not speak fluently in Telugu, even AP government initiated Telugu medium schools going to replace with English medium schools only, so majority of kids not able to speak and write in Telugu. The primary level children cannot easily understand several concepts better in English medium and cannot express their opinions and feelings better in English medium as compared to Telugu medium while switchover phase from first generation, later it can be tuned with second generation.

Pros:

Career of village background or Below poverty line pupils' career will get glow, get jobs easily in MNC Companies and it gives more benefits to their family growth.

They can go to abroad for higher studies easily by cracking IELTS, TOEFL and GRE which are primary eligibility criteria for MS (Master of Science), PHD in Foreign Universities.

9. **Just mention how did you feel about the English subject while in school----Easy? Difficult? If easy – in what way? If difficult-in what way? Because of grammar? Or because of spelling? Or because of sentence construction/ comprehension/ communicative skills? Any suggestions to tackle.**

   Ans: It is easy in grammar but difficult in sentence construction/ comprehension/ communicative skills. It will overcome by reading small stories, books, newspaper, watching and conducting debates movies in English.

10. **What is your opinion on English Question Banks/Guides sold in the market? Do you think they are helpful to students, apart from teachers teaching? Or are they harming the interest of the student (because they give the entire lesson in Telugu version, so that the interest to know what is in the lesson, while the teacher is teaching, is lost)?**

    Ans: I could say all these guides can help for grammar aspect but not in fluency. As per my experience fluency in English is possible by continuous interaction in English and correction by coach will give confidence to learners and overcome English phobia.

Name: Ganesh Nathi

Author Bio

Ms G. Indira (aka K. Indira) lives in Hyderabad. Now retired from Telangana Govt. Residential Schools, but when in service she found the teaching profession, not merely a job to do, but to dig out and reason out English Second Language (ESL) subject difficulties to schoolchildren. Ms Indira has an inquisitive mind and critical observation. In her relentless quest, she updated herself, although being in service, doing English courses like: PGCTE, PGDTE and M.Phil. from EFLU, Hyderabad, besides her M.A. in English literature and M.Ed.

As matter of habit, Indira diary-recorded the difficulties that students posed in ESL. She discusses them in one of the chapters of this book. While on deputation (2009-2014) to SCERT, Hyderabad, Ms Indira happen to work in the textbook-department and was also the author of textbook lessons for primary and high school classes of Telangana Govt. English textbooks. In addition to, she gave live-presentations of English lessons through SAPNET MANA T.V. This book helps English teachers in gaining background knowledge of Linguistics to teach English language. The book provides discussions on English introduction, English medium of instruction, bilingualism and multilingualism in English classrooms and also the latest trends on ELT from across the world.

Email - indira1051957@gmail.com